Ex Libris

St. Paul's Church

RICHMOND, VIRGINIA

Urban Church Breakthrough

Urban Church BREAKTHROUGH

RICHARD E. MOORE

and

DUANE L. DAY

Harper & Row, Publishers, New York

1370

This book is dedicated to

PAT AND LYN

CONTENTS

Preface

In the first volume (entitled *Russia Leaves the War*) of Ambassador George Kennan's study of Soviet-American relations, he tells of a series of strange events that took place on November 7, 1917. The scene was Petrograd, the seat of Kerensky's provisional government. On the previous night, the Bolsheviks, seizing power, had sabotaged the official government cars. Kerensky determined to leave the capital and seek troops loyal to him in order to suppress the Bolshevik thrust for control. He sent out an ensign to commandeer a motor vehicle with which he might search for loyal troops. In a scene full of chaos and confusion, the ensign finally located two automobiles in which Kerensky and his aide fled the city. At first the aide's car led the way, but no one in it knew where to go. Later the Pierce-Arrow carrying Kerensky jockeyed into first place and sped from the city at tremendous speed. A short distance outside of Petrograd, the car in which the aide was riding "ran into a rock" and was abandoned; the aide went to a railroad station, where he took a train. Kerensky, meanwhile, searched the countryside for troops and for the revolution that was occurring all around him.

This incident suggests the situation in which the Church finds itself in the era of metropolis. A revolution is occurring in our world. The Church and its leaders have shown a desire to be part of it. But at times the Church cannot seem to find the troops with which to do battle, and cannot even find the proper battles to fight.

The present volume begins and concludes with the assertion that the most significant external reality for modern man and his institutions, both secular and religious, is the contemporary metropolis. It further affirms that the Christian Church is honestly struggling today to minister in a revolutionary fashion to the men of metropolis, and to influence the forces which shape their lives. This book is all about that struggle, its tempo and scope, its failures and successes, and its significance for the renewal of the Church in the city.

Should the mood of the Church as it confronts the ever growing, often engulfing development of urban life be one of profound despair, anxious alarm, measured optimism, or euphoric rejoicing? Perhaps it should be a mixture of all these to do justice to the complex situation in which the Church in the city finds itself as the world moves toward the end of the twentieth century. To the degree that denominations are turning to the city with rekindled zeal to develop a relevant and revolutionary ministry, renewal is taking place. To the degree that they drag their ecclesiastical feet, renewal is only a fond hope for the future.

Whatever else one may say about it, the city is a place to which people have come. They have come from everywhere. In earlier days from the cities and rural areas of Europe. More recently from the rolling tobacco patches of Kentucky, the played-out coal fields of West Virginia, the crowded slums of Puerto Rico. They have come to find new jobs and new beginnings. They have come because the belching smoke of the city writes a promise across the sky.

The city is the place from which main-line Protestantism retreated—physically, mentally, and morally—during the twenties and thirties of the present century. As newcomers arrived at the center of the city, the older inhabitants, many of whom had a traditional Protestant background, spilled over into the suburbs. They packed up their churches and took them along. In the cities where these churches once ministered, there are as many people as there ever were. But now the ghost of a demolished church hovers over a parking lot; or the church building, still standing, bears the sign of some exotic sect on its door.

This retreat has not consisted simply of a withdrawal of residential congregation from the inner city. It has been marked by an increasing preoccupation with self-serving institutional programs, a separation of religion from the structures of reality, and a shrinking from encounter with the public and vocational world where the metropolis shapes its future. If the Church is the outpost of the Kingdom of God on the frontier of human need, thrust into urban life to witness and to serve, then Christians have much to account for. While the angel of the Lord has blown the trumpet for the charge against forces that confuse and depersonalize those who throng the city streets, the faithful have stumbled over each other in their retreat to a fortress farther out.

There are clear signs that this retreat has been or is being reversed—in the fifties, with the development of the Protestant Parish movement; in the sixties, with the employment of urban specialists, the assumption of responsibility by denominations for inner-city churches, the experiments in new forms of encounter with the "worlds" of the metropolis, and the general ferment for renewal that pervades all these activities and others unnamed in these pages.

Where do we go from here in the development of a total ministry to metropolis? The decision is plainly in the hands of the denominations. The direction is really the subject matter of this book, and especially the three middle parts: "Reaching Out from the Residential Base," "Frontiers of Ministry," and "Ecumenical Explorations in Metropolis." *Urban Church Break-through* is essentially an optimistic book. It recognizes a need: the Church must face the real world in which it now lives with renewed flexibility and openness. This volume explores what is happening across the United States as Churchmen put their faith to work in that world on which the church doors swing wide. It proposes that the denominations "must become the responsible agents of renewal through effective planning and administration"—a course they have already begun to take, as the book illustrates.

This study could not have been written without the patient endurance and persistent encouragement of the authors' wives through many late evenings and long weekends. Our secretaries, Miss Barbara Lohrey, Mrs. Sue Dlugokecki, Mrs. Eleanor Happle, and Mrs. Blanche Shields pounded the keys after hours to transform our scribbling into type, and so helped to make the book possible. There are many whose names are mentioned in the text whose gracious assistance in answering questions and whose helpful reflection on data were crucial in bringing the book to the light of day. Three men of the Church—Murray Drysdale, Lyle Schaller, and Peter Goodfellow—gave in an unusual way of themselves and their ideas to the production of this manuscript. In addition, thanks are owing to Milan Brenkus, James Campbell, Jesse Christman, Clarence Colwell, Dewey Fagerburg, Donald Koelling, Arlie Porter, George Todd, Bruce Whittemore, and David Zuverink, all dedicated ministers of God in this new age. Finally, special appreciation is extended by the authors to the staff of the Cleveland Presbytery of the United Presbyterian Church and the Central Atlantic Conference of the United Church of Christ, for the efforts in which they shared to transform this book from idea into reality.

PART I

Which Way to the Revolution?—An Introduction

The Search for Renewal

THE renewal of the Church in the contemporary metropolis cannot be resolved by naïve optimism or grand-sounding phrases. One of the writers was in Detroit several years ago listening to a denominational leader speak to a group of city planners and ministers concerning spiritual renewal in the city. The dynamic young church leader gripped the table and leaned forward for emphasis. "The Church," he said "is a revolutionary cell in American society." When the speaker concluded, the moderator of the meeting asked for questions. A layman standing in the wings spoke out. He said, "I've heard that claim more than once, and I've been looking a long time for this revolutionary fellowship. I do have a question. Where is it?"

The question "Where is it?" articulates a growing frustration within the institutional Church, which seems in many ways unrelated to the world around it. The Church appears to function in our society as a preserver of the best values of the past and as the promoter of a way of life set apart from the world. The prophets bring in minority reports, and official Church groups occasionally formulate visionary pronouncements, but the emphasis is on conservation rather than creation, disengagement rather than involvement, ritual rather than prophecy.

The problem is not simply the number of local church fellowships which invite people to leave their troubles in the sanctuary rather than meet the world there. Nor is it simply the scarcity of ministers who speak from their pulpits in specifics concerning our nation in bewildering technological and social flux—scarred by racial bigotry and strife, pitted with unemployment and poverty in the midst of widespread affluence. More adequately stated, the problem is that local congregations, ministers, and denominational executives; presbyteries, dioceses, and association committees; curriculum writers; national boards and agencies— do not consistently start from and return to the basic and overwhelming awareness that God is really acting in our urban society.

The love of God is to be found wherever life lies prostrate under the ugly foot of evil. God is involved wherever decisions are made that affect human destiny. The message and mandate of the Gospel directs the total Church to the place where God's love has long preceded us, wherever men are in darkness or conflict or need. The Church of Jesus Christ exists for the world, and not the world for the Church. And this world for which the Church exists is not some cosmic abstraction. It is the twentieth-century secular city, the place where men build and destroy, where they co-operate and compete, where they procreate and procrastinate, where they grow up, grow old, and die.

Renewal of the Church, when it comes, must touch the Church in all its expressions: the denominations, the ecumenical agencies, the local congregations and newer experimental ministries. Before illustrating the struggle for renewal that is taking place in the Church, and attempting to develop a set of appropriate organizational guidelines, it will be necessary to examine the climate within which renewal of the Church must flourish. This climate consists of the social milieu (the context of renewal), the thought-forms of the historic Church (the theology of renewal), and the institution of the Church itself (the source and object of renewal). To these in turn we must give our initial attention.

The Context of Renewal

IN one of O. Henry's stories two parties to a feud find themselves the sole survivors when the smoke clears away.[1] Bereft of relatives, Cal Harkness disappears from the Cumberland Mountains and gets a job driving an express wagon in New York City. A year later Sam Folwell, discovering his new place of residence, follows him to cancel out the Harkness clan once and for all.

Sam starts out on the New York sidewalks looking for Cal, his pistol strapped to his side and feud hate red in his eyes. He walks the busy streets all morning, darting nervous glances over his shoulder, fearful that Cal may be waiting in ambush behind a door or window to shoot him first. At noon Sam stands at the corner of a giant intersection. People rush at him from four directions. No faces turn toward him and no voices confirm his presence. Suddenly the foolish fear that he is dead and disembodied seizes Sam.

"Nobody can see me," he cries, as the city smites him with loneliness. There is no response.

"The Rankin's hog weighed more 'n ours," he shouts at a plump passerby. The fat man hurries on and buys a bag of roasted chestnuts to mask his alarm.

A club tickles Sam in the ribs. "Move along," says the cop. "You've been loafing here long enough." As Sam retreats across

[1] O. Henry, "Squaring the Circle," in *The Best Short Stories of O. Henry*, Modern Library (New York: Random House, 1945).

5

the street an automobile grazes his knee. A cab bumps him with its hubcap. The cabby purples the air with threats and profanity. A streetcar motorman clangs his bell and a newsboy joins the fray by pelting him with banana peels.

About this time Cal Harkness, whose work is over for the day, turns the corner. There, three yards away, he faces his blood enemy, the last Folwell, who has come to obliterate the last Harkness. Unarmed and unprepared, Cal wavers, but Sam's sharp eyes pick him out of the crowd. Sam rushes toward him and reaches—but not for his gun. He reaches for Cal's hand. "Howdy, Cal, I'm darned glad to see you." At the corner of Broadway and Fifth Avenue the Cumberland enemies shake hands.

Here is a parable of our life and time, a suggestive parable for the renewal of the Church in the metropolis. Written in the first decade of our century, the story is pure prophecy and basic myth. Here is the awareness that we are an urban culture in which rural values and methods of solving problems are no longer relevant. Here in the shorthand of storytelling are the migrations from farm to city and the problems of urban adjustment. Here is dramatized the opportunity to build new community in the all-pervasive environment of the metropolis.

The city is the basic fact of our American adventure. By the year 2000 there may be as many as 344 million people in America.[2] Eighty per cent of them will live in the vicinity of present metropolitan areas. At the turn of the century, when O. Henry wrote, three Americans out of four were rural. Now the situation is reversed, and three out of four are city people.

There is an irreversible migration from country to city, and a continuing migration from the core of the city to the swelling fringe, knitting cities together into metropolitan areas or regions. There is a less noticed but no less significant migration from the heartland of America to the coast. We are developing a strip city

[2] At present there are 200 million people in our nation. "If current trends continue, the U.S. population will total 249 million by 1980, and 344 million by 2000." *Population Bulletin*, February 1964, Donald J. Bogue, Director of Population Research and Training Center at the University of Chicago, in article entitled "Population Growth in the United States," p. 6.

along the west coast, another along the Great Lakes from north of Chicago to Erie, Pennsylvania; while the really massive strip city on the east coast runs from Boston to Washington, D.C.—identified, described, and named by Jean Gottmann in his monumental work, *Megalopolis*.[3]

Basic fact of our time in America: contemporary man in our country is neither rural nor small-town man. He is urban man. And because the city knits human lives together, because it is the matrix in which human destiny is shaped and molded, because it is the context in which the major battles of our century in America will be won or lost, those of us who call Christ Lord must take the city far more seriously than we have hitherto.

CRISIS IN COMMUNITY

The city can be seen as crisis, a continuing and ever changing crisis in community. There is a sense in which the impersonality and loneliness that overwhelmed Sam overwhelm us all—the feeling of isolation among masses of people, portrayed by Riesman in *The Lonely Crowd*.[4] The simple neighbor-to-neighbor identification of an earlier day is no longer open to the city dweller. There is a real question as to whether the urban psyche can bear depth encounter with the lives of the scores of people it meets in the crowded city environment.[5] The blasé mask of the city dweller, so objectionable to his country cousin, may be a necessary protection from the pressing crowd. The impersonal, contractual basis on which he conducts his business with semi-strangers, and the way he relates to other people as functions and roles rather than as persons, may be the only alternatives in a society where he can be cheated or betrayed by people he may

[3] Jean Gottmann, *Megalopolis* (New York: Twentieth Century Fund, 1961).

[4] David Riesman, *The Lonely Crowd* (New Haven: Yale University Press, 1950).

[5] See the essay on "The Metropolis and Mental Life" by George Simmel, reprinted in *Cities and Churches, Readings on the Urban Church*, Robert Lee, ed. (Philadelphia: Westminster Press, 1952).

never see again. Only in the intimate circle of the immediate family and the limited circle of close friends can the urbanized man toss his mask on the coffee table and become a person for others.

We cannot escape the problems of urban living by turning the clock back to our own version of the Cumberland Mountains. Mass-produced beer cans and pop bottles float down the old mill stream on a detergent foam. The dream cottage is furnished with chairs and tables made in Chicago and Sheboygan. Grover's Corners is only the click of a television tuner away from Metropolis, U.S.A. The city spills over into the countryside, swallowing up suburbia and exurbia and the farmland; the contemporary city cannot be escaped geographically or psychologically. And it may be seen as a crisis, ever continuing and changing, in community.

It is a crisis in black and white. What Silberman has identified in the title of his book is essentially an urban problem.[6] Our failure to achieve racial justice in earlier and more bucolic generations has assumed demonic proportions in the northern American city. Further, the color crisis is a crisis in education; the education of children and youth in the ghettoes of the city is inferior. It is a crisis in job opportunity; the Negro makes his bid for full participation in the American economy at a time when skill requirements accelerate and the tradition of work-for-income is threatened even for the hitherto privileged white worker. It is a crisis in housing. Every major American city has its ghetto where most of the Negroes live: the majority, because they could not afford decent housing even if available; but an increasing number who have crossed the income barrier solely because selective selling is a fact of life, as white homeowner and realtor combine in a quiet but colossal conspiracy.

Ultimately the crisis in black and white is a crisis in identity. The Negro child drinks with his mother's milk an "other" imposed self-image: to be black is to be different and second-class. A Negro from a deprived background may get an education and

<hr />

[6] Charles Silberman, *Crisis in Black and White* (New York: Random House, 1964).

learn the survival skills of his culture as European immigrants have done before him, but there is a difference. He is black, and judged by the majority accordingly. Doors of opportunity are nailed shut. Corridors of friendship have a this-far-and-no-farther sign.

Our culture has transformed a distinction of skin color into a deeply entrenched way of life. Is it any wonder that, increasingly, Negroes with reverse logic take the color of the second-class traveler as a badge and banner of superiority, striving as members of a group to win the right to act as individuals? In the American city the swelling protest is gradually turning into a politically oriented movement, especially viable as the Negro population approaches or surpasses a percentage majority in such cities as Washington, Philadelphia, Chicago, Cleveland, and St. Louis.

The city is a crisis in dollars and cents, a crisis for the community of men who traditionally have found dignity and meaning through work. People came to the great American city to tend the machines of the Industrial Revolution. Now their relationship to these machines has become ambiguous because of a second industrial revolution—of the computer and the automated, self-regulating machine. Contemporary technological change offers the promise of release from drudgery. What it also means is that, short of radical social readjustment, there is no place for the unskilled worker in our economy except as a consumer.

In contemporary urban culture the unemployed man has no acceptable self-image. This is because he has no status in the collective eyes of his family or his community. We discover who we are in part by the values that our peers place on us and our activities. The official rate of unemployment remained at or above 5.5 per cent during the first four years of the sixties. Unemployment rolls for Negroes run about twice the figure for whites, whatever their sex, occupation, educational level, or age. In terms of absolute numbers far more Caucasians are affected than Negroes or other minority groups and the burden of vocational obsolescence falls disproportionately on the aged, the handicapped, and youth entering the job market, as well as on the racial minorities.

Current welfare programs sustain life but not dignity. They encourage hostility in the strong and apathy in the weak. Ultimately the philosophy and application of welfare spells hopelessness for a permanently depressed class developing in our country, some 38 million Americans, the fifth of our nation that lives in poverty—and mostly in cities.[7]

Race and class are only two fragments of the broken metropolis.[8] In the generations ahead the relative significance, or at least the present configurations, of these two crises may change. Actually, the contemporary great city is a study in all sorts of denied fulfillment. For many city people life lacks the wholeness it needs and deserves. A man can be a saint at home·and a devil in the market place. Private values and public ethics are compartmentalized. The Church which in a simpler day made life holistic is wedded in contemporary practice to private and family values; is hesitant, unsure, and apologetic when it relates to the public or economic sectors of the city. Religion is usually thought of as a way of looking at certain things, rather than as a certain way of looking at everything. Birth and marriage, job and community responsibility, these are largely unrelated events or functions. There is no center of loyalty to which beliefs point and on which actions are predicated.

This crisis in communal wholeness is also a crisis in local gov-

[7] Figures from *The Triple Revolution*, p. 9, a pamphlet the text of which first appeared in *Advertising Age* magazine, April 6, 1964. The pamphlet, published by Ad Hoc Committee on the Triple Revolution, P.O. Box 4068, Santa Barbara, Calif., opens with letter to President dated March 22, 1964 and is signed by twenty-six prominent citizens from many walks of life.

[8] Although they are related, fragmentation is not an interchangeable term for specialization. Specialization degenerates into fragmentation through the apotheosis, absolutizing, or exaggeration of a distinguishable difference in life style, racial characteristic, ethnic background, vocational involvement, etc. Specialization *is* almost synonymous with urbanization. It has its origin in the psychological, geographical, and functional division between residence and work. As urbanization continues, the potential variety of work possibilities, residential styles of life, and leisure activities staggers the imagination. Trouble starts when these worlds become disconnected, as they have to a frightening measure in the contemporary metropolis.

ernment. The metropolis is broken into separate municipalities which overlap in services and jurisdiction. The suburbs offer an illusory way out of metropolitan responsibility and even bear names of rural nostalgia: Green Meadows, Rocky River, Glen Woods. There is a crisis in neighborhoods. The city is divided into vast homogeneous neighborhoods on the basis of race, income, ethnic background, and style of life. Too often there is mutual suspicion and little communication between them.

Thus there is a sense in which the city is a series of specialized worlds which tend to fly apart. Each develops its own rules and values, which often conflict even among themselves. For instance, Jonathan Smith can "accept" Negroes on his job and even in his church while "rejecting" them in his club and neighborhood. And because life is so effectively compartmentalized he may never really sense the contradiction.

THE NEW HUMANITY

And yet this is only half of it. To make this appear as the whole story would be to caricature a way of life that offers many satisfactions and opportunities for self-realization. The city is more than crises compounded one upon another: it is a challenge, and for many of its citizens a present fulfillment.

The words of acceptance Sam shouts to Cal above the din of the crowd point to the metropolis as a new creation, where men proud and free may join hands in true brotherhood. Perhaps it is only as we face up to our limitations and failures in community that we can clasp hands across the divisions of race and status and ethnic difference. The achievements of community in a rural agrarian or small-town society based on similarities of background and life style reinforced by the accident of isolation are limited and tribal. The basic pluralism of the metropolis challenges its citizens to build community on a completely new basis, and at the same time offers them the opportunity to do so.[9]

[9] The "new community" in the metropolis will of necessity maintain more anonymity and impersonality than did the tribe or the town. Harvey Cox

The city is really people all bound together in a bundle of life. Even in its most broken expressions it is an interdependent reality which affects everyone involved. Interdependence is and has always been the basis of whatever we mean by genuine community, and this is at least as real in the urban matrix as the fragmentation and divisions.

Ultimately the city is the tangible expression of God's intention for our humanity. Jesus' lament over Jerusalem (Matt. 23:37) is often interpreted as his rejection of the wicked city and all its ways, and by implication all cities. But we do not weep over our castoffs—we weep over broken dreams and unrealized promises; we mourn because what is and what ought to be are not the same. Jesus loved Jerusalem for its bustle and beauty, for the hallowed memories of the prophets who walked its streets, above all for the fact that God had marked it for special responsibility. If Jerusalem had not forsaken her destiny, how different history would have been! "Oh Jerusalem, Jerusalem, killing the prophets and stoning those who are sent to you! How often would I have gathered your children together as a hen gathers her brood under her wings, and you would not!"

Because it expresses God's intention for human community, the city, in the New Testament, is the central symbol of the Kingdom of God. The biblical drama of redemption begins in a garden, but—note carefully—it ends in a city. At the end of the ages the New Jerusalem comes down from the heavens and the City of God is with men. Human history is not consummated in the isolated self. The kingdoms of this world become the King-

---

(*The Secular City*, New York: 1965), in developing the theme of "anonymity as deliverance from the law," suggests that, in addition to the deeply personal "I-Thou" relationships, the urbanite enjoys many "I-You" relationships, which will never develop into true private relationships and yet are not simply "I-It" relationships. The "middle" relationships represent limitation rather than rejection. If characterized by honesty and mutual respect, limited and functional human encounters are not necessarily fragmenting or exploiting. The spectrum moves through family relations, camaraderie, vocational co-operation, sales and service contacts, to the briefest and most casual human encounters.

dom of our Lord Christ; His throne is in the midst of the City, where He reigns forever and ever.

And if it be true that the contemporary American city is dramatically different from that Holy City beside the crystal sea —still, the contemporary city is God's gift to us now as challenge and opportunity, the place of hope for the New Humanity, the context in which the Church of Jesus Christ can and must experience renewal in its total witness and service.

The Theology of Renewal

THE role of the Church in the metropolis, with its poignant failures in community and its challenges to build new community above old despair, is to witness through word and action to the Sovereign God who has entered into the stream of history; who, through His Son, became man; and who intends a New Humanity through His slain and risen Son.

THE HUMAN-SHAPED GOD

The Incarnation is the central doctrine of the Christian faith out of which all other doctrines flow. The Incarnation affirms that God sent His Son, that His Son became actual Man; that it was not the reverse—a man did not assume the attributes of God. True man and true God is the classic Christian answer to the question, "Who do men say that I am?" This formulation stands in stark judgment over those in any age who would see Jesus Christ as God *or* man. The definition of Chalcedon (A.D. 451) states: "This selfsame One [our Lord Jesus Christ] is perfect both in deity and also in humanness; this selfsame one is actually God and actually man, with a rational soul and a body. He is of the same reality as God as far as His deity is concerned and of the same reality as ourselves as far as His humanness is concerned. . . ."

Chalcedon may not explain the paradox of two natures in Jesus

Christ. It does preserve the paradox, that He was both man and God. Were the Council of Chalcedon to be held today, the contemporary statement concerning God and man in Christ would be expressed in terms of function and dynamism rather than the static ontology of Greek philosophy. But the paradox would remain. And it must remain. From the biblical perspective a great abyss exists between man and God because of man's sinfulness and God's otherness. This abyss could not possibly be bridged by man; but then God in the fullness of time sent His Son. The initiative was consistent with the love of God for man.

"The Word was made flesh and dwelt among us" (John 1:14). The entire history of God's dealing with His creation, in the great movements of history and in the lives of individual men, was brought to a climax when God graciously entered into the milieu of man in human form. To perceive, however imperfectly, that the man Christ Jesus was in fact the very Son of God, that the love He showed for His fellow men was the consummate expression of the love God has for all men—this is at the heart of the Incarnation and is at the center of the Gospel itself.

The "kindness and generosity of God" (Titus 3:4, NEB) enfleshed in Jesus Christ is directed to men—not universal, abstract, and generalized men, but men who hunger and thirst after food and righteousness, who labor long hours and play few, who are exploited, who are caught in the web of change and confused by the complexities of the problem of culture. In fact, this God of kindness and generosity shared these very conditions. In the person of His Son He entered this world of sin and death. He was born in poverty. He faced the human requirements of food and rest and relationships.

The message of the Church that "God was in Christ reconciling the *world* to Himself" means that God in Christ came not only to an ancient world of craftsmen, shepherds, and Roman legionnaires. The men of Megalopolis with their crises in black and white, in dollars and cents, and in community are recipients of God's gracious activity in Jesus Christ, an activity expressed through the Church but never limited to the Church. God can and does act in the events of secular history.

THE HUMANITY-SHAPED CHURCH

God shaped Himself according to the human condition; His Son took the form of our humanity that He might reveal the image of God.

Those who apprehended God in Christ became His Church. Paul refers to the Church as the Body of Christ. While this language of the apostle has been explicated in many ways, one of the meanings which may be derived from the expression is that the Church is an extension of the Incarnation. Even as Jesus Christ was the great expression of God's mission to the world, so, too, the Church is an expression of God's mission and is both human and divine in its totality.

As Jesus the Christ was the Son of God whether teaching, healing, praying, eating, or sleeping; so the Church as His Body is both human and divine in all its acts. There are times when its God-given mission and divine character are more obvious than at others—when the Church is celebrating the sacraments, serving the dispossessed, or pronouncing judgment on evil. There are instances, likewise, when the human dimension is only too apparent: when a budget is being balanced, a custodian hired, a furnace repaired, or a Sunday-school room painted. Nonetheless, in all this—in every facet of its life, throughout the range of its programming and housekeeping—the Church is His Body, human and divine.

As Jesus the Christ was neither man-in-general nor a Platonic idea of man, but a real and singular man; so, too, the Church of which we speak may not be seen in vague and general terms. There is a particularity about the Gospel, and there must be a particularity about the Church. If, in any way, our American denominations have ecclesiological significance (and who among the theologians would deny it?) then what has been said of the Church must be applied to the denominations. They, the Baptists, the Disciples, the Methodists, the Presbyterians, the United Church, are the Church in particular; they are both human and divine institutions.

All this is not a hymn of praise of denominations. American Protestantism, if it is to participate in God's mission to our metropolitan culture, must understand each of its decisions in terms of the human-divine nature of the Church. Its witness may not be confined to local congregations, concerned individuals, or something vaguely called "the Church." Denominational structures must see themselves as broadly based task forces for mission, and must develop a strategy for mission which is far more inclusive than the conventional tasks of overseeing and encouraging local congregations.

The Church cannot allow itself the luxury of promoting a kind of ecclesiastical subculture. It has been set by God in the midst of the world, to minister to the world in the language of men, using men as its instruments. In its way it is a thoroughly secular institution, which needs to accept and even have joy in its secularity. The best disciplines of man must be brought to its decision-making. The keenest insights of the social and behavioral sciences must be employed in its deployment of men and money.

At the same time, the Church must walk the razor's edge of its own dual nature. It must not speak in its own behalf, nor serve its own limited ends. It must embody the will and the spirit of its Lord. The Church must reach forth the hand of help to those in need because of the imperative placed upon it in Jesus Christ to serve in His behalf. The Church must embody in its own life the love that Christ embodied in His.

Renewal of the Church in the metropolis depends upon the expression of the divine-human paradox by the denominations in their corporate life. It has become fashionable to deplore denominations—to insist that renewal, if it comes, will come only through small groups or specialized ministries which flourish outside the camp of organized Christianity. The writers of this volume do not despair of the denominations. Rather do we despair of renewal without them. We believe it is the role of the

Church as the Body of Christ to shape itself according to the problems and potentialities of the humanity it serves in His behalf. And we maintain that the denominations as Church can do just that.[10]

[10] For an articulate presentation of a point of view different from that developed here, see Cox, *The Secular City*, chapter on "The Church and the Secular University." It is interesting that Cox sees hope in those secular bureaucrats, the organization men, and in their task force for secular mission, the organization. In what seems to be a contradiction he sees little hope in or for the Church bureaucrat and the administrative machinery of the Church.

The Source and Object of Renewal

RENEWAL will begin when denominational decision-makers set priorities, allocate funds, procure and place staff, and judge general effectiveness by an adequate understanding of the human and divine shape of the Church of Jesus Christ, an understanding fortified by the conviction that God is at work in the city where the Church is to witness. The recognition of the activity of God in present-day political as well as personal history is not a matter to be affirmed piously and then forgotten as the Church returns to business as usual. An awareness of the involvement of God must increasingly influence and determine the way denominations spend their money in the city. This awareness must affect the kind of Church-school curriculum our denominations write, the classes and varieties of people to whom they minister, the very nature of the ministry in which they engage, the types and goals of specialized and experimental ministries they develop, the criteria they use to choose their executive leadership, the theological training they give their ministers, and the standards by which they judge the over-all success or failure of their missionary endeavor.

At the metropolitan level Protestant denominations need to develop a total strategy for involving their financial and human resources in the mission of the Church to the metropolis. Certain inadequate conceptualizations have stood in the way of total planning for mission.

1. Mission has been divided by most denominations into self-supporting and aid-receiving categories. The denomination has assumed a tentative and sporadic concern for the latter only, doling out money without a clear set of priorities and goals. There are signs that this trend is being reversed, but it is still prevalent. The mission cannot be adequate if it is thought of as a deficit financing system designed to help financially embarrassed local congregations here and there pay their bills, even while it allows other congregations to abandon mission in areas of need and move into more affluent neighborhoods because those congregations are financially solvent. On the basis of an awareness of what God is up to, and an acceptance of the task God has committed to the denominations, where should these denominational families be allocating their resources and why?

2. Most denominations have fragmented the mission of the Church, entrusting "evangelism" to one national board or commission, "health and welfare" to another, and "Church and society" or "social action" to still another. The fact that these are all part of a single mission of the Church to the world, made in response to God's gracious outpouring, is obscured by fragmentation and departmentalization.

The full proclamation of the Gospel includes the spoken word, the preaching and teaching of the incarnation, death, and resurrection of Jesus Christ (*kerygma*); the fellowship of participation together in the encounter of Jesus Christ with the world (*koinonia*); and the expression of the Christian faith in loving servanthood to all men without distinction (*diakonia*). Words of faithful witness are incomplete without the ministry of service which validates the Gospel. Deeds of love and action are truncated without the preaching of the word and the redemptive fellowship of our Lord's Body. And any Church-promulgated word or activity at all is meaningless, without prior confrontation of the God who shapes Himself within the human structures of the world, as well as within the Church, to establish His reign of justice and love.

3. No conceptualization is more misleading than the persisting

one which insists that the local congregation is the only viable expression of Christian mission. The social realities of our day make pure congregationalism obsolete and ineffective in confronting existing problems which must be solved on a city-wide basis. Yet Protestantism still tends to be overly dependent upon congregational initiative, in a society so highly organized that congregations can be only part of the decision-making process.

Only as witness is broadly based—that is, as it grows out of denominational and ecumenical strategies—will it really penetrate to and influence the decision-making process that guides the metropolis. With increasing urbanization the Church must act through judicatories, associations, and dioceses which are metropolitan in scope, as well as through revitalized ecumenical structures, if the Church ever expects to develop a total ministry for the metropolis in which each local congregation has its own unique mission, and if it expects to have any pervasive influence upon secular society.

In a highly structured society the approach of the Church must not be limited to locally bound action without over-all policy, strategy, or program. The swelling cadre of professional staff hired by the denominations as metropolitan strategists, urban work directors, or urban specialists is one indication of the growing recognition that each congregation for itself in the city is simply not relevant. So also is the employment of survey and research specialists by city or state ecumenical agencies to develop long-range directives for the Church in its community setting. The effectiveness of such expertise depends ultimately upon the denominational policies that direct their labors. Is it their job to co-ordinate or supervise the same old institutional activities, only better, or to give guidance to the Church as it joins its Lord on new frontiers of mission and service?

The Church can be an instrument of God, participating in the structures of power where decisions are daily made. Or it can be an agent of bland reassurance, helping the disfranchised to be content in their misery and the affluent to be content with the status quo. The Church can be the probing conscience of our urbanized society, or a sanctified Shinto cult, blessing whatever is, as right. It can be an agent of social justice or a dispenser of voluntary—sometimes arbitrary, and often crippling—charity. It can be a force for unity through Him who breaks down barriers. Or by exclusive concentration on personal values and residential concerns, it can contribute to further fragmentation within individuals and among groups. The Church can be a fragile but effective embodiment of the New Humanity, a servant people who know the source of their deliverance; or it can be an ingrown club for the self-righteous. But short of genuine administrative renewal, individual experiments and demonstrations which attempt to tilt the Church in the "right" direction will be marginal to the mainstream of our highly institutionalized denominations, and will not really move the Church toward that revolutionary fellowship which our Detroit layman, in the meeting referred to on p. 3, had been seeking in vain!

PART II

Reaching Out from the Residential Base

Those who search as did our puzzled layman for revolution and re-newal stumble inevitably over that change-resistant rock: the resi-dential congregation or parish, the people of God who gather at stated times for worship, study, and recreation in a building called a church. The cries of impatience and frustration which follow this stubborn encounter suggest that, in many ways, this residentially based congregation as it now stands may be an obstacle to the God who is concerned for the New Humanity, rather than His chosen instrument.

Unwilling to write the residential parish off so easily, we have tried in the following pages to probe the role of the congregation on the corner as it struggles to reach out with relevance from its residential moorings. In the process of suggesting what it can be and do as a reality-shaped parish, we open the question of its adequacy as the one viable expression of Christian community in metropolis, and as the only effective vehicle for Christian action.

It is a long way in income, style of life, and sometimes in actual miles from the neighborhood of "the church farther in" to the luxury apartment environment described in Chapter 3, but the future of the residential parish is closely related to both as it endeavors to minister to the rainbow spectrum of people in metropolis.

CHAPTER 1

The Reality-Shaped Parish

ALTHOUGH generalizations are dangerous and frequently contradicted by exceptions, the established residential congregation deep in the city may be characterized as one which lives on past glory and is concerned with the specter of shrinking finances and membership. The congregation in the broad residential zone of the city or the affluent suburb, on the other hand, lives in the present and is concerned with maintaining and expressing its institutional strength. This is the congregation that contributes a disproportionate share of lay leadership and financial undergirding to the work of the denomination and the leadership of the city. The congregation still farther out, on the suburban fringe, lives for the future and is concerned with providing adequate building for a mushrooming membership. Whatever their institutional concerns, all three congregations share a common need: to develop relevant expressions of congregational life in metropolis. The issue can be simply stated: "What should these people of God be doing in the world, and how should they structure themselves for the task?"

But the issue cannot be dealt with as simply as it is stated. One school of criticism suggests that the congregation as we know it is too building-centered, program-centered, and minister-centered —isolated from reality in its pseudo-Gothic structure on a quiet residential street. The congregation is turned inward, promoting busy work for everyone from the kindergarten set to the graybeards. The church is financially introverted, raising money to support programs for its constituents so that they will be happy consumers and give more money to develop more programs. The extreme proponents of this point of view suggest that the residential congregation is irrelevant and must be replaced by a non-institutional expression of Christian community.

The minister-shaped congregation with the pastor at the center and the people revolving in a circle around him, assisting him in his ministry at "his" church, is certainly not an adequate shape for ministry in the metropolis. The building-shaped congregation where the minister is the master of ceremonies and the building is the scene where the ceremonies take place—where the goal is to keep the light on and the rooms buzzing with activities, and where the same people gather night after night in loyal membership groups and bemoan the fact that their ranks are thin—is only another version of the same irrelevancy.

But as long as people live in discrete units called families, and these families reside in little boxes called houses, and these boxes cluster together on concrete and asphalt strips called streets, the Christian Church will have to reflect residential realities in its ministry and program. The ministry of and to the local congregation desperately needs to be supplemented and extended, and this is a major concern of the present writers as we explore nonresidential ministries in the chapters that follow. While it certainly needs to be more relevant, it does not need to be obliterated.

Another line of reasoning suggests that the major denominations such as the Presbyterian, the Methodist, and the Baptist are suburban in orientation and membership, and that this is the basic problem. Rip the suburbanite out of his stained-glass security and involve him in the city church where reality is all around him—then he will discover the true nature and mission of the Church and his part in this mission.

There are several variations on this approach to discovering the relevant shape of the Church in metropolis. The metropolitan congregation may invite people who live farther out to stop "playing church" and take their membership farther in.[1] The associate membership idea is a halfway house. Belonging to the church in his own neighborhood, the suburbanite involves himself also in a congregation in a low-income neighborhood. Other variations on the same theme involve leaders from congregations throughout the city, or a quadrant of the city, in the development and execution of mission or interpersonal sharing across neighborhood and class lines.[2]

There is merit in developing cross-town experience among the members and leaders of residential congregations in various parts of a city. The metropolitan congregation with its extensive reaching out to all sections of the city—especially if it also has an intensive parish involvement in the neighborhood where it is located—is one viable way to bring some of the broken fragments of the metropolis together. But only as exposure and encounter lead further into the world for which Christ died is it justified. Contacts across racial and class lines must equip us for what Robert Frost has called in another context "a lover's quarrel with the world."[3] Busy work in suburban congregations, as Gibson Winter carefully points out, can be an expurgation of guilt—a way to relieve an uneasy social conscience by keeping its owner busy with "churchy" tasks.[4] The unwary suburbanite who involves himself in an inner-city church, planning or working for it

[1] Although a metropolitan congregation may have a neighborhood constituency, it can be defined as a congregation which draws members from a broad sector of the city or from the whole city. It is residentially oriented but not necessarily neighborhood-oriented.

[2] Gibson Winter, *Suburban Captivity of the Church* (Garden City, N. Y.: Doubleday & Co., 1961). Winter suggests a sector plan as the preferred approach to mission in metropolis (see section in his book on "The Inner City and the Inclusive Community"). As he outlines it, the sector plan is based more on neatness of theory than on the realities of denominational and interdenominational planning and sharing which differ from situation to situation. The cross-city adventure must be contextual, and by itself it is limtied in, i.e., it does not really break out of the residential box into the public and vocational structures.

[3] Robert Frost, "The Lesson for Today," from *A Witness Tree* (New York: Henry Holt and Company), p. 52. "I would have written of me on my stone: I had a lover's quarrel with the world."

[4] Winter, *op. cit.* See his discussion of "The Meaning of Activity," in chapter on "The New Religious Style."

or in it, can be caught in the same trap. Ultimately it is more important for the suburbanite to open up his own neighborhood to Negroes, to join in protest and change the structures which condemn a sizable segment of our society to inadequate housing, education, and work opportunities, than it is to teach in a Church nursery in a Negro slum. Racial injustice is only one of the many urban problems which the churchman must approach as citizen participant and not as worker in the institutional Church, if his ministry is really going to count.

Dialogue and exposure and worship and mutual acceptance are important. They are no substitutes for coming to grips with the issues in the society that create or corrupt. Neither the minister-program-building shape nor the cross-city shape is an adequate structure for the Church in mission. There is another shape, dimly seen, tentatively identified, and partially embodied in some residential congregations, which approaches adequacy. The hope of the local congregation lies in recovering the shape of reality, of human reality in all its richness and fullness.

The Church as Body

The basic affirmation of the New Testament is that God took human form in Jesus Christ. The New English Bible translation of Paul's Letter to the Philippians declares that the eternal Christ, not taking equality with God for granted, "revealed God in human shape" (Phil. 4:8). Christian faith proclaims that God poured Himself into human form to create "a single New Humanity" (also from the New English Bible, Eph. 2:15). Here is the suggestion that God is not ultimately concerned with religion or religious people. He is not ultimately concerned with ministers or buildings or Church programs or congregations. He shaped Himself into human life so that true humanity in its creative secularity could emerge.

Just as God took shape around and within human life in Christ, so the Church which is the Body through which Christ extends the Incarnation must take shape around and within humanity.

It must manifest itself as "the humanity-shaped Church." The central New Testament imagery of the Church as the Body is usually interpreted in a limited way. The emphasis is placed on Christians supporting one another in mutual interdependence, as the eye aids the hand and the head helps the feet. Seldom is the implication of the Church as Body fully developed. But the Church is the Body of Christ among men. The individual members complement one another in a mutual ministry to humanity which is more concerned with servanthood than with self-service.

The parts of the human body, as a matter of fact, relate to one another so that the whole body can fulfill a purpose beyond its internal relations.[5] The body is the way human beings confront the world, relate to the world, and exist in the world. This is the flow and pulse of life as encounter. The body is literally shaped by its confrontation with and involvement in the reality structures around it. There is a shape of the body for sleep and another shape of the body for love. These are not the same. The trunk and limbs and features assume one shape in greed and another in anger and still another in friendship. Depending on its situation the body bends and struts, leaps and stretches, extends or draws in on itself. And this process of responding to and taking pattern from the reality encounter is not peripheral but central to everything we mean by life in the body.

As the Body of Christ the Church does not exist simply for itself, for its own mutual interrelatedness. It exists to encounter the world, to take on the shape of humanity, and to be both bruised and exalted in the process. God's love for the Church is in every sense an instrumental love. God uses the Church to realize the New Humanity for whom Christ died.

This understanding of the Church as Body has profound im-

---

[5] Most of the Pauline passages which treat the Church as Body do highlight internal interrelatedness. However, in I Cor. 15:35-49 Paul puts Body in its broader context as the basis of life in this present world and in the Resurrection. For Paul the particularity of the Body (man, bird, fish, etc.) is inseparable from the essence of the creature as it relates to the world, and existence apart from the Body is inconceivable. The implications of this for the Church as Body are obvious.

plications for the residential congregation, implications which are seldom adequately explored or followed out. The basic role of the minister is not to persuade people to serve him or the building or the institution or even one another. The role of the residential congregation or any other expression of vital Christian community is not simply to turn out better ushers, Church-school teachers, and lay assistants to the minister. The goal is to develop better fathers and wives and factory workers and politicians and citizens, who draw basic insight and strength from the beloved fellowship of the Spirit. The residential congregation, like the specialized ministries to be described in later chapters, must take on form and extension where men pull switches and voting levers, push brooms and bowling balls. And as the congregation takes shape it exists in these situations just as surely as in the colonial structure on the corner.

Bonhoeffer recognizes four divine mandates which God has imposed on human beings:[6] labor, marriage, government, and the Church. These are the "given" of human life, the spheres where human existence is consummated in all its tragedy and joy; and all these mandates are sacred because all are of God. A somewhat similar frame is suggested by Donald Benedict of the Chicago City Missionary Society: the "worlds" of residence, work, leisure, and the public sector. The exact conceptual division of the world is not important; there are many ways to divide up the spheres of human activity and involvement. What does matter is that the congregation should take the world of humanity and its needs seriously as it shapes itself for mission.

Why not turn local church session, council, or consistory into a nominating committee which recognizes needs and recruits and develops task forces for ministries of service, study, and encounter? Why not give these limited-life commissions the same Sunday morning recognition and honor given to officers and Church-school teachers? And why not in the process disband the ongoing women's, men's, couples', and youth groups which first

---

[6] Dietrich Bonhoeffer, *Ethics* (New York: The Macmillan Company, 1955), section on "The Four Mandates."

exist and then look for tasks to justify their existence? It is interesting that when a Church group forms around a felt concern such as a building program rather than a membership organization based on an arbitrary age grouping, little time is wasted on the persistent question of "What are we doing here?" and "Why don't the others share our interest?" The writers have never spoken to a "knife-and-fork" men's club in a local congregation where at least one whispered apology was not made for the small turn-out.

The possibilities are endless in this approach to mission. For instance, the congregation can commission service-oriented task forces to participate in area councils, PTA's, and other community organizations; to visit mental hospitals and jails; to service tutorial programs and preschool nurseries. All that is needed is one person who senses the need, who may already be involved in the service project, and around whom the group can form. Rather than a single social action group in the local congregation, task forces for study and action can be formed around all the significant issues the congregation confronts in the public and residential worlds. Task forces can be created to handle less dramatic but still significant housekeeping tasks of the local congregation, such as the annual stewardship drive, the Lenten family nights. Even Church-school teachers may be recruited yearly, really a task force for Christian education of youth, a procedure one of the authors used successfully in a church he served.

Task forces move from involvement to reflection—with the reflection more loosely periodic rather than weekly or monthly —the minister offering theological and scriptural resources as the group seeks perspective on its involvement. The recognition of need and the recruitment of people to respond to it is easier for the local congregation when it is not programmed to death with membership organizations. This is why it is crucial not to superimpose the reality-oriented parish upon a conventionally busy congregation without first dissolving many of the organizations and self-perpetuating programs.

No specific task-force involvement should be pushed upon the members of a congregation. People are, after all, already involved in their worlds of residence, work, and citizenship. Program in the reality-shaped parish may often consist of no more than the pastor inviting parents or a vocational group together for a single evening to discuss the ministry they already have. And when a task force, beginning to question its present mandate, looks around for some new justification, it should be immediately disbanded to make way for a vital new claim on the energy of the participants.

Where the Action Is

Does the reality-shaped parish actually exist in any congregations? In a measure, yes, although it is usually found in a mixed and ambiguous form.

Bethany United Presbyterian Church on the near west side of Cleveland, frustrated with the proliferation of organizations without end, established three commissions responsible for all the activities in the local congregation. All three commissions are accountable to the session (the governing board of the local congregation), a number of members of the session are on the commissions, and the commissions are free to recruit members from the local congregation.

The first commission is called the "local commission." This has the power to create, recruit for, and in the end dissolve task-oriented committees which deal with the internal and institutional life of the local congregation: stewardship promotion, Christian education, music and worship, and pastoral care. A second commission is concerned with the "community." This holds the greatest promise for fresh creativity; within the first six months of operation it had recruited a group of people to relate to the urban renewal program projected for the general neighborhood of the church, and another group to sponsor a preschool nursery for the parents of working mothers, a service needed in the neighborhood. The third commission has as its object the "world." This commission is concerned with general missionary education and special benevolence offerings. It makes a nice balance with the other two commissions, but will obviously meet more sporadically, deal more in generalities, and involve fewer people.

The Church of the Saviour, a widely publicized congregation in Washington, D.C., is structured on an unusual integrity and intensity of personal commitment. Six study courses embracing a year of training precede membership. Following his internship the applicant must prepare a forthright statement as to what Christ means to him, and what specific disciplines for the Christian life he intends. As part of his statement of intentions he promises to "be a contributing member of one of the groups." These groups, called by the congregation "mission groups," are really a version of reality-oriented task forces.

In a sermon in the spring of 1958 Gordon Cosby, pastor of Church of the Saviour, said, "This is all you mean by a mission group: Two or more persons who have been grasped by the same concept of God's task for them, and who have been grasped by God."[7] The mission groups really grew out of fellowship groups developed early in the life of the congregation and represent a move from inward intensity to outward service, a discipline for members of the congregation which supplements those of prayer and study. Mission groups exist for a threefold purpose: to nurture members, to serve, and to evangelize. Every member is expected to participate in at least one group. Groups come into being when through prayer and exploration members of the congregation expose a need which calls them to service.

Mission groups at the Church of the Saviour are involved in various kinds of world encounter. The Potter's House, an outstanding example of a dialogue ministry, is sponsored and staffed by a mission group. There is a mission group which takes responsibility for the Renewal Center, an agency for counseling and medical care located in a farmhouse on a 175-acre tract in Maryland owned by the church. Here recovered alcoholics and

[7] Elizabeth O'Connor, *Call to Commitment* (New York: Harper & Row, 1963), p. 49.

the emotionally disturbed find a halfway house between the impersonal drabness of the mental institution and the overwhelming demands of a normal environment of work and residence. One group participates in the Potter's House workshop, a lively experiment in the arts which affirms the lordship of Christ over the world of sculpture and painting. A mission group is currently engaged in a program designed to meet the scholastic and intellectual needs of youngsters in a slum neighborhood, by supplementing the grossly inadequate library facilities of the Washington public schools. Still another mission group is involved, with similar groups in ten other Washington congregations, in a project called FLOC (For Love of Children). The thrust of FLOC is to find homes for the children in Junior Village, an overcrowded, understaffed institution for homeless children. The goals are twofold: to find or establish foster homes for emotionally starved children, and to empty Junior Village so that it can be used as a psychiatric center for disturbed youngsters.

"The policy of our church, reaffirmed by the session every six months," said Ray Swartzbach, the dynamic pastor of Calvary Presbyterian Church in Detroit, "is to keep the lights out and the building locked." He went on to explain, "God is incognito, working out there in the world, waiting for us to get out of our Church buildings and get in tune." New members at Calvary Church are urged to assume three basic obligations. The first is to attend worship regularly on Sunday morning, the second to support the church financially, and the third to make a conscious commitment to an agency or work involvement as a Christian outside what Swartzbach calls the denominational base. This third charge and the way it is implemented is the key to the uniqueness of Calvary Church.

For one thing, by deliberate intention there is almost no conventional programming in this congregation. A Church school, a women's group left over from the "old days" when Calvary was an all-white congregation of 1,800 members, and two youth groups which meet one hour a month each are the only membership organizations featured on the calendar of this six-hundred-member metropolitan congregation, which now numbers as many Negroes as whites among its constituency. A church member cannot immerse himself in institutional busy work. No opportunities are provided.

For another thing any service program initiated by this congregation is undertaken because of an unmet need, and because the church is free to experiment and to demonstrate in a way other community agencies are not. As soon as a private or public agency will do the job the congregation phases out. For six years Calvary conducted the largest youth canteen in Detroit, serving nearly 600 young people of the streets—the so-called "handkerchief-head kids" that nobody cared about reaching until this church pioneered the way. During all the time that twenty-six laymen of the congregation conducted and chaperoned the canteen, they and other members were appearing before city recreation agencies, pleading for adequate services. The best field house in the city was built as a result of their efforts, and now reaches and serves these long-neglected young people. The church-sponsored canteen—no longer needed—has been discontinued.

The real thrust of the witness of Calvary is the emphasis on lay involvement outside the walls of the church building. Members are expected to take the suggestions and convictions projected from the pulpit seriously and to put them to work where they laugh and love and live. If they are "winged"—an expression used by the pastor for the snipe-wounds of painful circumstance or encounter—they are to stagger back and a small group will form around them to help them heal their wounds. At the point of genuine encounter the difficulty of witness becomes apparent, and the real growth and learning take place.

On the positive side some thirty to forty members of this congregation are consciously involved in putting their convictions to work, and discuss their dilemmas regularly with the pastor, who —because he is not program director of an eight-day-a-week institution—is able to visit all his members at least annually. Several church members are actively involved in CORE; one member, at the head of a government agency, calls Swartzbach every time he appears before the city council; three schoolteachers struggle to make sense of secular education; and several members of the congregation who are domestic workers try to understand and mitigate fear in the white community where they work.

On the negative side, the majority of the congregation really do not understand why the church does not sponsor more teas and family nights. And in seven years of de-emphasis on program and emphasis on involvement in the secular circles of society, only two groups have formed as a result of a crippling encounter. In one of these a woman's house was stoned. She was the first Negro in an all-white neighborhood. When she asked for help, members of the congregation, both Caucasian and Negro, went to sit with her in her living room and watch neighborhood hostility through her window on the world, sharing her perspective in order to strengthen her witness and theirs.

Across the years Calvary has initiated and "floated out" a tutoring program adopted by the Detroit school board, and a clinic for third offenders before the law. At present church members are involved in three *ad hoc* committees, really issue-centered coalitions involving other community organizations as well as the church: one concerned with job discrimination, one on education, and one dealing with local school problems.

Ray Swartzbach refuses to romanticize or to overemphasize results, but he is convinced that, "if anything is going to happen in the Church it will have to happen in this kind of way." Although these three churches—Bethany, Calvary, and Church of the Saviour—are quite different in their approach, they are congregations that have moved beyond what one inner-city pastor calls the "Mickey Mouse" of congregational life to a serious reinterpretation and reshaping of their mission. Calvary Church in particular, which one of the writers has followed with interest since attending a Thanksgiving service in 1956, when the first Negro family appeared for worship, is developing a ministry which the secular society in Detroit takes seriously, and from which the ecclesiastical pattern-makers of standard brand denominations can learn. Churches like these are on the frontier of whatever tomorrow the residential parish will have in metropolis U.S.A.

In summary:

1. The problems of our urbanized society must be met and solved within the economic, political, and social systems by which that society is governed, where the challenge and crisis of the metropolis comes to focus, and where God is now at work.

2. The churchman as a participant in that society and its systems has his own special ministry to perform in an intricate network of personal, vocational, service, and community relations.

3. The continuing education of the church member for this responsible ministry must be seen as a central task of the Church.

4. The reality-oriented congregations which equips the member individually and as part of a task-oriented group for his ministry in the world is a proper form, or shape, of the Church for ministry in the metropolis.

5. Educational efforts of the local congregation may need to be supplemented by specialized ministries that require professional skills not available in the residential congregation—that focus on metropolitan issues and structures, offer a level of group interaction the residential congregation cannot provide, and can be as legitimate expressions of Christian community as the residential congregation.

CHAPTER 2

The Church Farther In

THE besetting temptation of the congregation "farther in," the congregation in a low-income transitional neighborhood which has been stranded—left to "imagine its past and remember its future"—is simply to serve its dwindling membership rather than its changing community. It is a temptation to reject the shape of reality, preferring that of institutional self-service. The tragic consequences of this usually unadmitted and unrecognized spiritual solipsism are reviewed in the following pages, along with suggested steps by which the process can be reversed, several examples of inner-city congregations which *are* ministering to need, and a commentary on the role of the denomination as partner in renewal.

PROFILE OF DEATH AND RENEWAL

Scene 1. The library of Uptown Church. Some twenty-five people, most of them over fifty, all Caucasian, and none residents of the predominantly Negro neighborhood around the church, are listening with obvious apprehension to a younger man who is speaking. Tension crackling in his voice, the representative of the metropolitan unit of the name-brand denomination of which Uptown is a member congregation breaks the bad news.

"We know you people of Uptown Church have tried. So have those of us who represent the Association. We know that some of you have called on the people who live around Uptown Church. Many of you feel that if we would only give you a minister and continue financial help you'd be all right. But the decision has been made, and our Mission Committee is going to recommend to the Association that this congregation be dissolved after Easter. The building will revert to the denomination and your letters will be forwarded to the church of your choice."

Scene 2. Same place, the library of Uptown Church, one year later. Except for a scout troop meeting in the basement, the church has been vacant for almost a year. The roof has leaked and there is a thin layer of plaster dust on the Bibles and hymnals that lie on the floor and on the piano, where they were left by the congregation when they vacated the building and locked the door. Two men are standing just inside the library door. One of them is director of metropolitan mission for the Association, recently hired to co-ordinate its urban involvements. The other is a young man fresh out of seminary and newly ordained. He has just been called by the Association to organize a new congregation in this old building. Plaster dust swirls around their feet as they finish the inspection of the library and leave the room.

As they start out the front door of the church and down the steps, the two ministers see a neighborhood woman contemplating a new sign proudly planted on the well-trampled lawn—a sign promising A NEW CHURCH TO THE GLORY OF GOD. The woman turns as the church door swings closed. "So you are going to start up church again." She pauses. "I think that's wonderful."

Scene 3. Three more years have come and gone, and the scene is the same, the library at Uptown. Only now there are bright chintz curtains on the windows, the walls are freshly painted, the books and hymnals are dusted and in their places on the shelves. An entirely different group of men and women from those present four years earlier are sitting in the library. For the most part they are younger; they are smiling rather than apprehensive, and most of them are Negroes.

This is an important evening. Representatives from the Association are having their annual conference with the officers of this three-year-old congregation. The preliminary business is over and the pastor is presenting his report to the strategy subcommittee of the Association Mission Committee.

"Sunday attendance is at 150, and communicant membership is pushing 200. This year we expect to raise one-fourth of our current expense budget of $28,000." The minister reviews his own work and that of his professional staff: the young director of Christian education who also guides the community-center program sponsored by Uptown Church, and the part-time calling pastor, a retired minister who visits in the community three afternoons a week. Having highlighted the newest program additions —a maternal health clinic, ongoing classes in "Negro History," a preschool nursery, and a "Right to Read" program for illiterates —he concludes, "At Uptown Church we're happy to join with the Association in ministering to this neighborhood."

REFLECTION ON THE PROFILE

We are not suggesting that the only way to minister in the city is to close out problem churches and start over. Nor do we believe that every congregation farther in can be as statistically successful as the new one at Uptown. This case history was chosen because it clearly illustrates many of the elements involved in administrative renewal in one crucial area of total mission to the metropolis: the inner-city residential parish.[8]

1. The in-city church can't go it alone. It needs the guidance and support of the denomination of which it is member.

2. Guidance and support should be given by the denomination before it is too late. To be effective, support should bolster inherent strength rather than compensate for inherent weakness.

3. If a denomination expects to begin new churches it must be willing to discontinue others where the ministry is not needed, or where the situation is beyond repair. The existence of a building or a loyal remnant is insufficient justification for the con-

[8] All the churches in this chapter are drawn from life and are churches with which the authors are familiar.

tinuation of a congregation. Most denominations are not willing to admit this, and therefore temporize and postpone until desperation forces their hand to action.

4. The primary issue in aiding a church in the "middle" of the city is not the survival of a particular institution, but responsibility for ministry in a particular situation.

5. Main-line denominations can serve changing or difficult neighborhoods when the motivation is witness and service rather than the perpetuation of a dying institution.

6. Money doled out by a denomination to a weak, ineffective, and poorly planned ministry is wasted. Money adequate to provide competent staff and full program can be dramatically effective.

7. Proper ministerial leadership is crucial in effectively ministering in the city. An encouraging sign is the number of young men coming out of seminary who see the inner city as a frontier of service. The church in the inner city does not have to be a dumping ground for incompetents.

8. The in-city church must not run a conventional building- and membership-centered program. Ministerial leadership and laity must identify with neighborhood needs and aspirations, participating in the organizational life of the community and offering building and staff resources to the community. In its situation the church must be a "reality-shaped parish."

9. Denominationally based urban specialists with special responsibility for liaison between the denominational unit and the inner-city church in the areas of staff, budget, and program can play an important part in effective ministry.

10. Above all, the mission in and through the local church must be understood by the local congregation involved as a partnership in mission with the denomination.

Many of these principles of administrative renewal will be expanded in the Conclusion of the present book. Meanwhile this needs to be stated categorically: The future of our Protestant witness in the metropolis is at stake in the church "farther in." The crises in black and white, dollars and cents, and personal and communal fragmentation afflict the people who live in inner-city neighborhoods more acutely than in suburban communities where main-line Protestantism is at home. These people matter to the Lord of the Church, who is in the city beckoning His Church to follow and to serve, to express the oneness of the Body of Christ across the divisions of urban life, and to embody the New Humanity for whom Christ died. Unless the Church is willing to minister where statistical response is less than overwhelming, it must settle for a fragmentation of its witness and structure.

A City with Many Faces

Any comprehensive look at administrative responsibility by denominations for the inner city must begin with the recognition that there is not one inner city or one kind of inner-city congregation. Uptown Church, featured in the "profile of death and renewal," is located in a lower-middle-class neighborhood where the majority of residents are family people living in single dwellings. Largely populated by Jewish people through World War II, the parish area of Uptown became in the fifties one of the more desirable neighborhoods open to Negroes and changed rapidly into a predominantly Negro community. Uptown continues to change—the demolition of neighborhoods elsewhere through urban renewal forces a circumscribed Negro population to crowd into Uptown, breaking down zoning regulations and causing anxiety among the present residents, many of whom wish to move away from the threat of incipient blight and lower-status newcomers. This new church development in an old building must continue to change and minister to change or it will become as irrelevant as the congregation that preceded it.

Housed in a huge basilica on a treeless, windswept corner, Intown Church is the only main-line Protestant church in an irregular rectangle of the city two and a half miles long and a mile wide. This is known as a Roman Catholic section of the city—79 per cent according to a study made in 1954—and most of the people are southern and eastern European in ethnic background.

A growing number of southern whites in the area are a prime target for evangelism and service. This community of low- and modest-income people turns over slowly, probably because of the high percentage of first- and second-generation Europeans who like their neighborhood, homes, and ethnic solidarity.

In a community setting where prospects are scattered and scarce, Intown Church has ministered for seventy-five years. Across the last twenty years membership has hovered between three and four hundred members. Surprisingly enough 45 per cent of this congregation live in the immediate area. Family ties, loyalty to their pastor (who at sixty has spent all but three years of his active ministry in this congregation), and a sense of shared mission draw others back from the in-lying suburbs. The pastor of Intown Church has been willing to subsist on a substandard salary and has given himself to the neighborhood and the people for over thirty years. What will happen to the congregation when he retires is an open question which most members don't like to think about.

At times Intown Church members have been discouraged with their lonely stand. Their denomination has not been especially helpful until recent years. During one period of low finances a denominational executive told them that they might as well close up shop, and although the sentence of death was pronounced a decade ago and never carried out, it is remembered with bitterness by some members. Now the denomination pays the salary of a part-time youth worker, and congregational leadership sees the denomination as helper rather than threat. In an interview the pastor of Intown Church assessed the situation this way: "Opportunities have always been before Intown Church, which is the only Protestant church in this wide area. We have not imported suburban members for their own sake, but for the sake of the community surrounding the church. We have suburban members vitally concerned with the inner city. We find problems to be a spur."

Fartown congregation shares facilities with a large and well-staffed neighborhood house located on the edge of a public housing project. Although this congregation numbers less than a hundred members it draws the majority of its members from public housing (a rare situation among the major denominations). Fartown faces an unusual dilemma as an institution concerned with self-perpetuation. Success for its members means that they move away from the church both physically and psychologically. Indeed, the dilemma is even more profound. The adaptability which enables people to participate in the group life of this congregational unit of a major, middle-class-oriented denomination usually means that they are able to "escape" public housing. So from the very beginning the more involved church members are just passing through. Within two or three years after uniting with the church they move on to private housing.

Insofar as the pastor and officers of Fartown are willing to accept the role of enabling upwardly mobile people to move away from public housing and their congregation, they can achieve success. Insofar as they judge themselves by the statistics and financial standards of middle-class congregations they can expect to experience only failure. Fartown congregation will never be a large, self-supporting congregation. Most of the people it counsels and serves will never belong to the membership or attend public worship. The children and youth who constitute the majority of participants in worship and activities can never support the congregation financially. The unemployed half of the adult membership can make only token contributions. Yet here is a vital church with excellent lay leadership—a church reminiscent of the congregations of New Testament vintage to which not many mighty or wealthy were called.

Downtown Church is based in a storefront on the shabby edge of the center of the city. Here are the cheap eating houses, the third-class hotels, and the small industries that frame the central business district. Although families are scattered through the area, living in apartments above storefronts and in frame buildings in the shadows of smoky factories, the neighborhood is visibly the "turf" of transient single men of all ages and dispositions.

Downtown Church is supported by an interdenominational

missionary agency which is sponsored in turn by some seven major denominational families. The minister belongs to one of these supporting denominations, but Downtown Church is affiliated with another.

The make-up of the congregation is even more interesting than the complex ecclesiastical relationships. Three "subcongregations" participate in Downtown Church. The working nucleus of the church is some twenty-five elderly men and women, the remnant of a great metropolitan preaching center which in its day was the largest and best-known congregation in the city. When the "Mother Church" could no longer operate its fortress-like building and elected to disband, a stalwart little group of members decided to remain in the neighborhood, affiliate with the missionary society, and begin a ministry to the immediate community in a storefront. The second subcongregation—very few of whom are actual church members and most of whom are objects of mission rather than initiators—is drawn from the transient men who live in the neighborhood. The third subcongregation is recruited from the youth of the community, for whom the capable young pastor of Downtown has a genuine liking and who return the compliment.

The unusual ministry of Downtown Church is illustrated by an experience of the pastor with one of his three congregations. One night a gang which included members of the Downtown youth group broke into a huge warehouse which stock-piled imported compact cars. When the boys had collected enough money to feed gasoline into four or five cars, they turned the warehouse into a speedway, dashing around packing boxes, bouncing bumpers, and smashing fenders. Leaving the place a shambles, the joy-riders crept home in the early morning hours. Then one young man, troubled in retrospect, confessed the nocturnal drag race to the minister of Downtown Church. The conflict between privileged conversation and social responsibility was resolved by the pastor in consultation with his friends among the guilty. He persuaded the group to assume responsibility for the damages, without losing their trust or alienating them from himself.

As a membership organization Downtown Church is a manifest

failure. As a specialized ministry, a kind of neighborhood chaplaincy with a residential base, this church ministers effectively in its unusual environment.

SIMILARITY WITHIN DIVERSITY

Uptown, downtown, all around the town, communities differ and churches come in a multiplicity of sizes, shapes, and problems. But however the situations may differ, the churches "way in" confront similar challenges which their denominations must help them to meet, often giving subsidy, always encouragement and support.

Many churches in the midst of the city are located in neighborhoods where low incomes and chronic unemployment accentuate the problems all families face. In such situations the counseling burden increases in proportion to the inability of neighborhood families to finance an adequate ministry in their midst. In many instances, neighbors of the church in the city may lack the traditional skills which make for strong lay leadership in congregational life. Specialized professional staff skills which the local congregation cannot afford are needed to develop a program suitable to the community, and to equip the saints for their leadership roles.

The neighborhood of the city church is often characterized by poor housing, overcrowding, exorbitant rent, crime, prostitution, and other marks of the broken community. Caught in an environment it can neither control nor escape, the city family may be deeply scarred. The church in the neighborhood must seek wholesome community change whatever the cost to local congregation and supporting denomination. This commitment to change is extremely significant. Without it the church in the city becomes a kind of zoo without bars. And the denomination which undergirds it becomes a spiritual zoo-keeper, willing to pay the price to keep the captives content with their lot, but not willing to let them be really stirred to that significant social change which is polite longhand for the phenomena of peaceful rebellion and revolution.

CHAPTER 3

High Hopes for High Rise

THE BIG BOOM

NO exploration of the relationship between residence and ministry in the metropolis would be complete without some observations concerning the Church and the apartment house. During the 1950's, residential building in the American city consisted mostly of new single-family dwellings in the suburbs. There are still a million such new houses built across the United States every year. But since 1956 the number of new apartment units started annually has quadrupled, and the apartment share of new units has grown from a nominal 9 per cent in 1956 to 30 per cent of all new construction in 1963. The trend continues into the last half of the sixties—insofar as the home-building business mushrooms, the *growth* has been in apartment buildings.[9]

Apartment-house units come in a variety of sizes, prices, and packages. The luxury apartment units ($65 to $100-plus per room), and to a lesser degree the middle-income unit ($25 to $45 per room), especially when the unit is packaged in a high-rise building, have been the kinds of apartment units that have attracted most attention from the churches. By a conservative estimate there existed in the summer of 1966 at least twenty ongoing experiments and projects sponsored by denominations,

[9] David Seligman, "The Move to Apartments," *Fortune* (April 1963), pp. 99–101, 221–26.

ecumenical agencies, and local churches related to high- and middle-income apartment-house living.

Many of these apartments are going up in the heart of the city. As part of an effort to draw the suburbanite back from his exile outside the corporation limits, the apartment offers him instant city, with shopping, commuting, and entertainment advantages. But the apartments are also proliferating in the old, inlying suburbs that ring the incorporated core of the city. Here tired old homes are being torn out and replaced by apartments designed for people who want suburban living but do not want to make the long trip in every day from a little bungalow on the outer edge of a sprawling metropolis.

All apartment units do not rise high above the city smog. In fact, until the early sixties most high-rise apartments were six to eight floors, handled by one elevator; or eighteen to twenty floors, serviced by two elevators. Now only gravity and imagination set the upper limits, and some towering apartment units are miniature cities, replete with shops and offices as well as dwellings, all in a single tremendous spire.

For the nontechnical purposes of this chapter a high-rise apartment is a luxury (or middle-income) rental building high enough to be serviced by an elevator.

THE INACCESSIBLES

When the Rev. Benton Randolph was engaged by the Presbytery of Cleveland in the spring of 1964 to carry on a pilot ministry to people who live in private high-rise apartments, one Cleveland pastor, reflecting on all the doorbells to be pushed, commented, "He'd better be all thumbs." The popular picture that emerged in the minds of the general churchgoing public, reinforced by the local newspapers, was that of an elevator-riding clerical cowboy rounding up the strays in the vertical canyons of the city. The heading on one front-page article in a Cleveland paper made this image explicit: MINISTER LOOKS FOR LOST SHEEP ALONG CLEVELAND'S "GOLD COAST." And because the

Presbytery and the United Presbyterian Board of National Missions (which underwrote most of the program) were not sure exactly what they expected from this two-year project, the circuit-riding, doorbell-punching projection has never quite disappeared.

Misconceptions concerning an exploratory ministry to the so-called luxury high rise are really based on an oversimplification of the challenge the high-rise way of life presents to the Church. "How can the pastor 'call' in high-rise apartment areas where people are (*a*) seldom at home, and (*b*) behind locked doors and intercoms?"[10] This question superficially outlines the basic problem as inaccessibility. The door in the front of the lobby is locked. The doorman stands guard. The residents are gone during the day. The caller must introduce himself through an intercom and may be met with disinterest or even hostility by the voice at the other end. How in these circumstances, pray tell, can the high-rise resident be reached, and how can he be delivered to the church?

Inaccessibility is really a secondary issue. High-rise living to be understood must be recognized as a specialized style of life in metropolis. As suggested earlier, urban living involves specialization—both requires it and makes it possible. In itself specialization is productive. It leads to fragmentation only when the cement of community and personal wholeness, or both, are missing. Specialization is a fact not only in the worlds of work and leisure; it is also a fact in the realm of residence, and the high-rise apartment is one dramatic example.

The high-rise dweller has a limited liability in his surroundings. He has paid for convenience, privacy, extensive physical services, and usually for proximity to good transportation. He is not anchored to place or neighborhood in the conventional sense. In a study made of residents in an upper-income apartment area in Chicago, personal interviews indicated that "few of them know

[10] *Christian Century* editorial, "No Solicitors Allowed," February 10, 1965, pp. 165–66. The quotation is a summary of statements made by frustrated ministers as they confront the world of high rise.

much about the community in which they live. They do not know the names of local streets, the names of elementary schools, or the ward number, and often they are not aware of the name of the community in which they live. . . . There are relatively few children so that the neighborhood tie of a local school has little application. . . . They have not, of course, established roots in the community through real property ownership."[11]

Obviously the high-rise style of life raises the question of whether geographical proximity is always a basis of community, and if it is not, whether it ought to be—and if it ought to be, whether it possibly *can* be. Value judgments about the high-rise life style are most negative when the person passing judgment is convinced that real community must be equated with spatial proximity.

Not only does the high-rise phenomenon represent a particular style of life; it is related to the stages of life itself. The high-rise private apartment is deliberately designed to serve the first and third stages of adult living: the unmarried or prechild period and the postchild period of maturity and retirement—the "empty-nest" phase of the human adventure. The pressures and opportunities of urban living make these nonfamily styles the "freedom stages" of life. As the number of people increases who are reaching or approaching retirement age *as couples*, and as these couples experience the relative freedom and affluence that come when there are no longer children to guide, support, and educate (one out of four families in 1965 were "empty-nest" families), the high-rise style of living will become an increasingly popular option.

The traditional residence parish weaves many of its activities around the interests of people engaged in raising children; has greatest statistical success in reaching "family" people who live in individual homes which they are buying; is largely out of touch with young singles and couples in the first "freedom stage"

[11] Quoted from *The Church and the Apartment House*, p. 18, a pamphlet published by the Division of Evangelism, and the Department of the Urban Church, Board of National Missions of the United Presbyterian Church; undated but distributed in 1964.

wherever they may live; and does not usually recognize as a special group those who have entered the second "freedom stage." In this context, what does a high-rise style of life shaped to the relatively unencumbered stages of life say to the ministry of the Church?

Until the high-rise apartment boom of the sixties, ministries concentrated on the cliff dwellers considered primarily the physical problems of contacting residents, not the stage and style-of-life factors. The Chicago Methodist Temple, a combination apartment house and cathedral, attempted to redeem the apartment world by owning a small part of it. Local churches surrounded by the spires and towers of high rise, eager to recruit members from these encroaching "skymarks" (combination of skyscraper and landmark),[12] and frustrated because the apartment residents were both hard to reach and to recruit, developed explanatory brochures and calling campaigns from outside the building and its ethos.

In the sixties a new approach has been developing, one which Benton Randolph in *The Cleveland Edgewater Apartment Experiment* describes as "reflective presence." This approach involves more listening and less preaching—more of a reaching into the world of the high-rise dweller than an attempt to pull him out of it. Significant pioneer experiments include:

1. A specially designed new church development for an urban-renewal, high-rise neighborhood in Washington, D.C. (Rev. Alfred Shands, III, Episcopal, begun in 1961).

2. A Council of Churches resident representative in the Borough of Queens, New York City (Rev. William R. Mowalt, Methodist, 1963).

3. Resident clergymen, free from all institutional responsibility, to listen and to learn: in New York (Rev. Raymond Scott, Presbyterian, 1963); in Chicago at the publicized Marina City

---

[12] Term used in article "The Place Called Winton" by Stuart Abbey, in the *Cleveland Plain Dealer*, Home Magazine Supplement, October 18, 1963, p. 3.

Towers (Rev. Roy Blumhorst); and in Pittsburgh the first ecumenically sponsored man (Samuel Craig, Jr., Presbyterian, 1965).

4. A catalyst for community action, business management sensitivity and responsibility, and the self-evaluation of residents, in Cleveland (Rev. Benton Randolph, Presbyterian, 1964).

The high-rise frontiersmen are of a common mind that inaccessibility is not so much a major problem as it is a nuisance for the unimaginative pastor. The pastor can reach his parishioners in high-rise apartments by calling or writing them in advance; or by adapting his schedule to their life style and calling in the evenings or on Saturday. The outsider who has paid for privacy can be reached on an ecumenical basis. Already under way in two cities and projected in a third is a "religious resources" program. The process is simple. A retired layman, preferably living in a high-rise apartment, and better still if he works in the apartment where he lives, is engaged to visit non-church-members under an ecumenical umbrella: Protestant, Roman Catholic, and perhaps Jewish. The first time around he visits everyone, then only newcomers. Potential prospects are classified by religious preference and referred to the appropriate congregations for follow-up. Residents are less resentful when they do not have to confront a series of purely parochial callers. Apartment-house managers are more sympathetic to an ecumenical approach. The parish priest or minister saves time and avoids hostility when he is contacting a person who has indicated interest, rather than merely an apartment number and a name.

The issues raised by the style of life and the stages of life of high-rise inhabitants are more profound. There is the gap between the interests and needs of the freedom stages and conventional parish life. There is the whole question of whether the "worlds" of work, recreation, and public service are not communities where, in fact, young adults and adults whose children are grown live more intensively than in the "world" of residence. The local congregation usually seeks to involve people in its ongoing program. How can it involve itself in the lives of those who do not readily respond to its program, shaping itself around their needs and interests, bringing the Gospel to bear on their real concerns? And if the congregation on the street corner cannot adapt, what new form and focus of ministry must be developed for the apartment dweller, either in the apartment house or in the work and leisure communities? For example, coffeehouse ministries are one approach to reaching the young adult in the sector of lesiure and recreation rather than the residential context.

The unique challenge of high-rise living to the Church is one clear example of the inadequacy of pure congregationalism in the total ministry to metropolis. An effective strategy for high rise must be developed and executed on a broader basis than that of the local church. Current experimental ministries developed by denominations can continue to serve effectively as listening posts, sources of insight into what is becoming a clearly defined way of life for a substantial minority of urban people. Beyond experimentation certain choices have to be made, and implemented with staff and financial resources, by the denominations and ecumenical units responsible for urban mission. Resources of money and manpower must be put to work, or the Church will be shut out of the high-rise apartment by forces far more powerful than locks and buzzers and desk clerks.

Based on developing insights into the needs and opportunities of people in the freedom stages of life, and especially the latter stage when children are grown and gone, the denominations must decide where the focus of ministry to high-rise residents shall be. Is the neighboring residential church the place? If so, those churches which cluster around high-rise apartments must be encouraged to develop programs which both challenge and meet the needs of both the young and the older adult, and also develop on an ecumenical basis realistic plans for recruiting high rise dwellers into their congregations. Are the apartments themselves the place—i.e., are the freedom stages of life in the high-rise apartment so specialized that the local congregation with its family orientation cannot minister effectively, and the gathered fellowships must therefore shape themselves within the walls of apartment buildings? Or is the whole focus on residence a mistake and the high-rise apartment a world of limited involvement for the dweller—a place where he hangs his hat and coat and lays down his tired body at night, while his "real" life goes on elsewhere in vocational activities, leisure-time pursuits, and community involvements? Attempts to form apartment-house churches have not been statistically successful. Is this because the denominations have not really put their resources behind new Church developments designed exclusively for high-rise dwellers, or is it rather that the apartment dwellers are reluctant to involve themselves in the lives of neighbors with whom they share little beyond proximity?

The Significance of Residence

Designed specifically for the second freedom stage—when the children have grown up and gone away—the new communities called "Leisure World" developed by the Rossmoor Corporation may eventually provide as much opportunity for insight into contemporary Church needs as the high-rise apartment experiments. Intended for, and limited to, people fifty-two years of age and older, there are now three Leisure Worlds in California, one in Maryland just outside Washington, D.C., still another in New Jersey, and land is being assembled to develop another in the vicinity of Chicago. These developments vary in size from the New Jersey community of 45,000 residents to 18,000 in the Maryland project. Residents who live in housing apartments, four to eight units in a cluster, buy shares in the community as well as equity in their homes.

In the New Jersey Leisure World a religious council is responsible for overseeing an ecumenically oriented ministry. On three separate campuses, carefully located in this planned community, nine sites have been set apart for denominational Church buildings. These buildings are intended for corporate worship only. On each of the three campuses there is an ecumenical fellowship hall for through-the-week Church activities.

Whatever the future of Leisure Worlds and "new towns" such as Columbia, Maryland (the community for 150,000 people projected for the southern extremity of Megalopolis, between Baltimore and Washington), there will be more diversification in available housing rather than less in the city of the future. Already the tract home, the split-level, the condominium, the town house, and the four-family flat are among the viable alternatives in metropolis, where increasingly people are able to choose housing adapted to their income and the style of life they covet for themselves. Even the ghetto tenement and the apartment in the public housing project fit this frame. Through a series of decisions, some overt and some quietly taken for granted, society has decided that people with financial problems shall live in certain places under certain specialized conditions.

As the Church struggles toward a total ministry to metropolis it must take diversification in residence seriously, but not naïvely or blindly. The significant issue for ministry and renewal is not the kind of building but the sort of people who live in it, their concerns and their needs. The container is not the man. The building has significance for ministry in metropolis only so far as it influences a pattern of life, expresses a style of life, and draws to itself people with similar backgrounds and burdens. Is ministry to young adults really more difficult—significantly different in quality and kind—when they live at home than when they cluster in high-rise apartments? Questions like these need some thinking through if specialization in residence is to be kept in proper perspective.

PART III

Frontiers of Ministry

"The Church is an Army that has been sent on a mission. In order to accomplish its purpose, it must have a base; and in order for it to have a base, it assigns certain troops the task of building and maintaining the base so that the rest of the army may be free to do its job! We tend however to forget the Church's mission and wastefully assign most of our people to building and maintaining bases with the result that we do not accomplish its true purpose. More members need to be assigned to, and trained for, the true work out in the world where the conflict between life and death goes on unceasingly."[1]

Problem raised by Reuel Howe in his perceptive word-picture of the Church as an army which overstaffs its barracks: How shall the Church get off home base? It needs not only to recognize the responsibility to move its members out; it also needs programs and techniques that work. Certainly for the foreseeable future the residential parish is home base, the place where the troops are recruited, trained, and sent into the various sectors of society. And beyond question the base of family and residence has an integrative function, tying the worlds of work, public life, and leisure together, giving wholeness to the specialized and departmentalized roles played by individuals and groups in metropolis.

However, it is increasingly obvious that the residential parish is limited in its capacity to shape itself within all the divisions of life in metropolis, even when it tries; the farther removed the battle from the familiar surroundings of home and neighborhood, the greater the straining to relate, and the less the competence of the local pastor to serve as a resource-theologian. It is in this sense that the ministry of the local parish needs to be supplemented and extended.

When the troops are called out of the parish they are brought together around issues, within public and vocational structures, and in the context of leisure. Nonresidential ministries on these three front lines, together with the kind of community organization that thrusts soldiers of Christ into conflict with secular powers and principalities, constitute the subject matter of the following four chapters.

[1] Reuel Howe, *The Creative Years* (New York: The Seabury Press, 1959), p. 222.

CHAPTER 4

Organizing for Change

TO the suburban church member of a major denomination the kind of community organization which promotes militant protest in slum neighborhoods swings in an alien orbit. His home, whether modest or a mansion, is amply protected from undesirable encroachments by strictly enforced zoning regulations. The interest rate on it is 6 per cent or under, and less than 20 per cent of his gross income goes into buying shelter for his family. If he is not the proud owner of an incinerator and a garbage disposal unit he can count on the week's accumulation of waste being whisked away by the village sanitary unit. A well-paved and politely policed street runs by his front door and opens onto a well-subsidized throughway, which delivers him ultimately to an upholstered chair in the air-conditioned office where he spends his working days. The plumbing works in his bathroom, and he does not have to share these popular facilities with neighbors down the hall. His children go to a school where French and trigonometry and advanced-placement English are in the curriculum, and when they finish public high school, the college of their choice awaits them. He may have to borrow on his life insurance to see them through, but no sacrifice is too great for the kids. Here, in short, is man with the power to realize within limits the style of life he desires for his family and himself.

Oh, sometimes he feels powerless and overwhelmed by big labor, big business, and especially big government; more personally threatening is the big boss on the floor above him in the office, but somehow he manages to beg, borrow, or benefit from power when he needs it. For example, last year there was a proposal to run an expressway through his suburb, eliminating a lovely municipal park and several houses, including his own. The county commissioner had no problem in getting clearance for the expressway in the core city. The homes to be cut out were already slated for demolition as part of an urban renewal project, known cynically in some circles as Negro removal. Clearance was not so routine outside the city limits, where our suburbanite lives. Photographs popped up in public buildings all over his suburb, showing the expressway sprawled across parks and homes and schools like a huge python. Pamphlets describing the threat and suggesting ways to block the proposed artery were available in his suburban supermarket and bank. An *ad hoc* citizen's committee went to work, with the backing of mayor and council, and every political decision-maker involved in the expressway from governor to county engineer was deluged with visits and phone calls, offering clubs and candy as part of the protest. Needless to say, the expressway is now diverted—and our suburbanite was part of the power process that diverted it!

It is virtually incomprehensible to the suburban church member who does not think of himself as an especially influential person that there are thousands of people in the filthy, fetid slums of the city where he works who, because of race and background, are excluded from birth until death from the powers, privileges, and opportunities which he accepts as naturally as the air he breathes—that these people see him as member of a system which holds them in a kind of polite slavery—that the style of life he takes for granted is a candy store into which they can see but cannot enter. The worlds of the affluent and the alienated meet but do not often merge, and there is little real communication between them: on the same commuter train, one of the writers recently heard two women in front of him talking about their trips to Europe, while two others behind were discussing their caseworkers and the lateness of their welfare checks.

Whether or not the suburban church member understands or accepts the proposition, the reality-shaped parish in low-status and minority-group neighborhoods has a responsibility to the people who are emasculated by the compounding social crises identified in the opening chapter of this book. And one of the really effective instrumentalities for this involvement is neighborhood community organization. Community organization is simply participating with people and their neighborhood institutions in the process of self-determination and significant social change.

CHANGING THE SCENERY

The justification for community organization is concisely stated in a paper endorsed by the Department of Social Welfare of the Chicago Church Federation, a statement which dovetails with the basic orientation of this book.

The Church participates in local community organization because the people of God are in this world as the Church. . . . It is the world which he came to save; it is the world in which the Gospel is proclaimed and enacted. . . . A Church which neglects its mission to the world is not only unfaithful in its calling as the people of God, but in fact ceases to participate in the life and ministry of Jesus Christ in the world.[2]

Implication and imperative: The major denominations through their local congregations have a role to play in community organization. The congregation in a corporate sense as well as through its membership should participate alongside block clubs, businessmen's clubs, PTA's, and other groups in the solving of community problems. The staff and the resources of the local church should stand behind an alert citizenry engaged in the process of self-determination. Decent schools and housing, adequate standards of zoning and sanitation and police protection, are the business of the Church. It is not enough to change individuals and leave the environment untouched. The Church

---

[2] "The Local Church and Community Organization," p. 1, a position paper prepared and adopted by the Department of Social Welfare of the Chicago Church Federation, October 1962.

must be party to a process which changes the context in which individual lives are shaped.

There are profound implications in the process of genuine self-determination in a community where people have long felt powerless, and as a consequence have been apathetic concerning the possibility of altering their status and style of life—suspicious of the "branch offices"[3] of organizations which are in the community but not of it: main-line churches, YMCA's, and an assortment of volunteer welfare agencies. When Saul Alinsky, executive director of the Industrial Area Foundation, and the best known champion of the conflict school of community organization, describes the dignity in which a man clothes himself when he discovers that his life situation can be changed through participation in an effective community program; his face glows like an Old Testament prophet. The slum dweller no longer has to be helpless; he can now be an initiator rather than an object of compassion and charity. He may not have the power of position and money, but he has the power of numbers, and through the organization he has a voice in what happens to his community, his neighbors, and his family. Because he has the power to protest, influence, and when necessary threaten with boycott, embarrassment, and the vote those whose power is utilized to maintain the status quo, he will be able to tilt the total direction of the metropolis in such crucial areas as integration and employment. "The bridge from black to white is green—the color of the American dollar."[4]

The local church and community organization have become a topic for debate largely because of the ongoing romance of Protestants and Catholics alike with Saul Alinsky of the Industrial Areas Foundation and the hard-nosed philosophy of community organization which he espouses. Tilting their lances against this

---

[3] Term used by Nicholas Von Hoffman, supervisor of the Woodlawn Project, in a paper, "Reorganization in the Casbah," prepared for Board of National Missions of United Presbyterian Church, November 15, 1961.

[4] Quoted from a speech by Saul Alinsky to the National Association of Intergroup Relations officials, Great Lakes Regional Conference, June 22, 1962.

outspoken advocate of community conflict are Harold Fey of the *Christian Century*, who sees Marxist overtones in Alinsky's program, and the Rev. Walter Kloetzi, Lutheran executive and metropolitan strategist. Joined in the battle on Alinsky's side is *Fortune* editor Charles Silberman, whose book *Crisis in Black and White* devotes its whole last chapter to a description and positive evaluation of Alinsky's aggressive methods in Wood-lawn, a vast, substantial slum on Chicago's South Side; and Dan Dodson, director of the Center of Human Relations and Community Studies of New York University, whose approach to community organization and action closely parallels that of Alinsky.

The man around whom the battle swirls, messiah to his advocates and Machiavelli to his foes, appreciates the contribution his critics are making to the future of the Industrial Area Foundation. Part of Alinsky's tactics is to have an identified enemy against whom the troops can unite; so much the better when the enemy volunteers. "Fey is the best friend the Industrial Area Foundation has," he commented to one of the authors. A large, graying man in his middle fifties, Alinsky, who has many strong opinions, which he is happy to expound at length, fits the classic definition of a cynic, an idealist who has experienced disillusionment with the world. He is a man of seeming contradictions, a Jew who considers Paul one of the two outstanding community organizers of all times (the other is Moses); a realist who builds his organization upon an appeal to self-interest, even as he exudes an almost sweet and sentimental passion for social justice.[5]

The fervor with which his critics attack Alinsky is more difficult to understand than Alinsky's philosophy of organizing for change. Not really appreciating the extent of fragmentation in contemporary urban society, and not really recognizing the existence of a depressed subculture, an alienated urban proletariat, his detractors do not see the necessity for radical reorganization in the slums. Of course they also object violently to the nature

[5] See Marion K. Sanders, "A Professional Radical Moves in on Rochester," *Harper's* magazine, June and July, 1965, for an exposition of Alinsky's personal philosophy based on taped interviews.

of the reorganization and its guidelines, the organizing principles of conflict, power, and self-interest. These three concepts are the key to Alinsky's community organization program. They are also closely related, willy-nilly, to the future direction of community organization, whether in Alinsky's style or any style; as well as to the future of the civil rights movement, the community action phases of the government-sponsored "war on poverty," the issue- and structure-oriented ministries described in the following chapters, and the over-all role of the Church in the contemporary metropolis.

Self-Interest

"The community organizer digs into a morass of resignation, hopelessness, and despair and works with the local people in articulating (or 'rubbing raw') their resentments."[6] Here is where the community organizer for the IAF newly arrived on the scene begins. Alinsky sees the process as a cathartic, turning resentments outward rather than inward, where they corrode and corrupt. Self-interest, coupled with the possibility of effective remedial action, is the motivation to which appeal is made. The specific goals of individuals and groups are meshed: one person supports another in his demands, so that he in turn can be helped to get what he wants.

This leader has been sharply criticized for his lack of idealism and his unabashed appeal to selfishness. To this Alinsky replies that any other approach to mass community organization is unrealistic and naïve. The writers agree with him. The suburbanite sketched in the opening paragraph of this chapter acts in his political and economic and residential "world" largely on the basis of his self-interest as he conceives it. The fact that he considers his interest to coincide with those of the general public is incidental, and in many cases quite mistaken.

[6] This quote and the brief quotes which introduce the commentaries on controversy, conflict, and power are from a speech by Alinsky to the Chicago Chapter of the National Association of Housing and Development officials, January 29, 1962.

This organizing principle, as espoused by the IAF, simply says that the self-interest of the slum dweller also needs to be recognized and implemented. There is a real sense in which the realization of the needs of ghetto dwellers is in the public interest, especially if one believes that the general public is best served when through the clash of interests come negotiation, reconciliation, and a new power situation in which the interest of the Haves is no longer imposed on the Have-Nots. The question is really this: How is social justice achieved? The labor movement of the thirties redistributed economic power and benefited the general public, although without question both labor and management were fighting for their own self-interest—a self-interest usually narrowly conceived.

A community organization is not the Church of Jesus Christ. Groups and individuals participating in community organization can be as altruistic in their motives as they are willing and able. A sense of serving can impel a local congregation to involve itself in a neighborhood organization. Even here self-delusion is a constant danger. Men of commitment can be open toward the future, responsive to high-sounding challenges on the basis of unselfish self-giving; only the self-righteous explain past conduct apart from self-interest.

Kloetzi, an articulate antagonist of Alinsky, charges that the Roman Catholic Church has been involved with the IAF in projects to keep Negroes out of some areas and confined to others. Robert Christ, a Presbyterian pastor involved through his congregation in the OSC (Organization for the Southwest Community), one of the IAF projects in Chicago, suggests another way of looking at Roman Catholic involvement. In a thorough report on his personal and local church involvement he wrote in 1961: "Because the renewal of the community demanded interfaith cooperation there has been the necessity for joint action. Again, driven together by the world, the 'separated brethren' of Christianity have been compelled to remember they are also brethren . . . the common basis which both Protestant and Catholic have in Christ and in the Church Universal has supplied the foundation for cooperative action."[7] Mr. Christ's assessment of motivation does not sound like narrow self-interest selfishly conceived and executed.

CONTROVERSY AND CONFLICT

"Issues which are not controversial usually mean that people are not particularly concerned about them; in fact by not being controversial they cease to be issues," says Alinsky. The executive director of the IAF believes that conflict and controversy are essential to successful community organization. Buried resentments must be exposed, articulated, and directed toward those who prefer to dictate the process of change in society on their own terms. Significant change and conflict go together—like love and marriage in the song of a few years ago, they cannot be separated.

Dan Dodson of New York University suggests that what he calls the "power order" works through "integrative processes" as contrasted with "conflict processes,"[8] the latter being the approach of the IAF. In the integrative process those who share the decision-making power—the titular community leaders—come to a polite consensus as to what is best and then publicize their conclusions through their public relations media of radio, television, and the newspapers, whose directors are usually part of the

[7] Robert Christ, "The Local Church in a Community Organization," October 1961, p. 7. This is a mimeographed case history of the involvement of a Presbyterian church in community organization, covering period from January 1959 to October 1961.

[8] *Social Action* (United Church of Christ publication) article, "To Work Effectively as Agents of Change" by Dan W. Dodson, February 1965, pp. 26–27. "Power order" points to a loosely structured leadership in metropolis which "rules" by the reflection of general public opinion and the formulation of new consensus opinion rather than on fiat. There is no handful of "power elite" who make policy in the "back rooms" of the large metropolis. Rather there are numerous constellations of power which establish allegiances around specific issues on the basis of what can be paradoxically termed public-spirited self-interest. A partial list would include, typically: the welfare or community chest establishment, business community leaders, industrial barons, foundation staffs (who distribute patronage for business and industrial groups), communication directors, labor elite, politicians, and the real estate interests.

power establishment. The process is one of consensus rather than conspiracy, and is generally accepted as the normal way the metropolis moves. The conflict school challenges the assumptions of the decision-makers, confronting community leaders with goals significantly different from their own, questioning the altruism behind the decisions made by the "power order" and insisting on being part of the decision-making process.

It seems obvious that people who are advantaged—who either participate in or benefit from the decisions made by the "power order"—do not usually initiate certain kinds of change until these are brought to their attention or even forced on them by those who suffer from the status quo. The suburbanite sketched in the opening section of this exploration of community organization is no better or worse than the man in the slums; he is in a different life situation and guided by a different philosophy, with a different goal set. His conscience can be reached and his actions changed only by forces outside him. First, his presuppositions must be challenged; then the reasons for the pressures put on him must be interpreted—one role of the reality-oriented church located in the more affluent neighborhood. Whether Alinsky would put it this way or not, the greatest favor that can be done for the well-meaning suburbanite is to challenge him from a position of power. He may be then able to concede what in some cases he has wanted to grant all along. And the concession is acceptable because it comes in response to a demand rather than as paternalistic largess.

Those who hold power in the social order prefer to "win them one by one," i.e., assimilating into their social and economic milieu those individuals who are religiously, racially, and culturally "outside" but are ready and able to participate according to the unwritten rules laid down by those issuing the invitation. The system works better when differences between the "in" crowd and the "out" group are minimal, when the agony of those outside is not too acute, and when there is easy access up the ladder of affluence, during a time when the job market is expanding and there is room not only at the top but on every rung. The invitation to "join us if you can" leads only to frustration in a complex urban situation like the contemporary one, and to resentment of the "Uncle Toms" who have gone over to the opposition.

The power order really offers middle-class values without also offering opportunities—genuine and not theoretical—to go with the values. "Conform and we will give you a chance," invites the power order. The group who have adopted the tactics of conflict answer, "Give us a genuine chance and in our own good time and way we will conform."

The "enemy" identified, exposed, and challenged by mass community organization is really twofold. Outside the camp are the unscrupulous real estate agents, slum landlords, and politicians who allow slack enforcement of housing, sanitation, and zoning codes; the police who appear to the slum dweller as an "army of occupation"; and, more removed but no less threatening, the vast number of affluent city dwellers and suburbanites who perpetuate ghetto living, joblessness, and inadequate education in the slums by their inaction and silent acquiescence. Within the ghetto itself is the other compound enemy: apathy, hopelessness, acceptance of segregation as a way of life; lack of political acumen. Alinsky believes in organizing the dispossessed to fight both foes alike.

POWER

"The only reason people have ever banded together in the past, present, or future, is so that through organization they can create a power instrument with which to implement or realize their desires or needs or their program." Alinsky applies his analysis of the relationship between power and organization to labor unions, political parties, and religious groups which organize to convert others to their beliefs, as well as to his own kind of community organization. He feels that power should be recognized openly and honestly as an ingredient in human relations. To disguise it, to dress it up with euphemisms or pretend it does not exist, is to engage in basic dishonesty.

In respect to a realistic approach to power Alinsky has theologians like Reinhold Neibuhr and John Bennett in his camp. Bennett makes an important distinction between covert and overt power.[9] Those who have power in the social order use it unobtrusively but nevertheless effectively. In the private world they can evict tenants and discharge employees; in the public arena they can bypass fair housing ordinances and refuse to apply zoning regulations in neighborhoods they have written off as hopeless. Above all, covert power is expressed through inaction and delay. The power of the Haves to protect interests which they publicly present as the common good can be more coercive than the power of a mass community organization. The power is just more polite and less obstreperous.

Those who derive power from money, job situation, status in the community, or all these have no trouble finding expression for their hopes and aspirations. Not so with the disadvantaged who are the subjects of community organization in low-income neighborhoods: minority groups, the unskilled, the uneducated, and the newcomer. This suggests that freedom from domination by white society will only come when the disfranchised in the Negro ghetto have the power to demand it. Received simply as a gift it cannot be accepted because it is psychologically destructive.

An important part of Christian social responsibility is to give political and economic power to victims of social injustice. Alinsky's methodology is one viable approach to the redistribution of power. The goal is to enable people to become part of the decision-making process. This cannot be done on an individual basis. Hence, mass community organization, which utilizes the power of a large number of people acting in concert.

Identification with power has far-reaching implications for the

[9] *Christianity and Crisis* article, "The Church and Power Conflicts" by John C. Bennett, March 22, 1965, p. 49.

self-image and sense of worth of the individual. In the early pages of this book the writers suggested that the crisis in black and white is ultimately a crisis in identity, a sense of rejection and powerlessness which traumatizes the young Negro in the slums. There are no strong and successful male figures in his immediate experience with whom he can identify in order to counteract his low self-esteem. He is crushed under a self-fulfilling prophecy. He does not produce because he is not expected to produce, and he accepts with apathy the judgment imposed on him. What he needs is to be linked to a process which, by encouraging and enabling him to stand up and fight successfully, will infuse into him the manhood he has been denied. The ultimate hope is that he will become equipped educationally and psychologically to participate as a free individual in a society which has excluded him on a group basis, and which he can re-enter initially only as part of a group.

Fears that Alinsky will tie together his neighborhood associations into a monstrous power organization and take over a city like Chicago seem largely hysterical. Alinsky has little interest or skill in organizing the affluent or even the lower-middle class, who in his words are "too fat." The real danger is that in communities like Woodlawn, where the IAF has been at work, the organization will lose its edge of anger and concern because of a measure of success.

Through 1964 the IAF had organized in four communities in Chicago, and had engaged in extensive work among the Mexican laborers on the West Coast. The next year saw a major expansion of the arena of operation: new thrusts into cities such as Buffalo, Rochester, Kansas City, Detroit, and Syracuse. The reasons for the extended scope are apparent. Ghetto riots and near-riots in northern cities during the summer of 1964, climaxed by the violent upheaval in Los Angeles in August, 1965, are eloquent testimony that the problems of a depressed racial minority can not be wished away. To churchmen and others, Alinsky seems more and more like a man with a viable alternative to blind rebellion on the one hand and inaction on the other. In Syracuse the major mover was the University; in Rochester the Council of Churches. In Detroit Protestant and Roman groups are supporting the IAF on a consultative basis as it guides organization in the inner city on the West Side of the city. In Kansas City the "sponsors" have been Episcopalians, Presbyterians, and Roman Catholics.

Organizing campaigns got off to slow starts in Buffalo and Kansas City, in the latter case because Alinsky, overextended with his many invitations to action, could not furnish organizers until January of 1966. In Buffalo the urban committee of Buffalo Presbytery brought a recommendation to the presbytery to support the IAF. Two elders, lay officers of local congregations in the presbytery, responded with a suit under a New York statute which forbids the use of Church funds for secular purposes. The legal battle seems headed for the Supreme Court.

Syracuse, where IAF has been at work since 1965, has had its traumas, too. The government, using antipoverty money, made a $314,000 grant to Syracuse University to teach slum organizers with Alinsky as the part-time "professor." When city hall realized it was one of the targets, mayor and housing authority vehemently protested use of government funds to stir up class warfare.

On April 12, 1966, the Presbytery of San Francisco of the United Presbyterian Church voted to borrow $200,000 to bring the IAF to San Francisco. Projected plans include a Community Organization Institute as well as a community organization project. Across the years Alinsky has trained only eight organizers in depth. The Institute will enable him to expand his training program, and Alinsky is planning to supplement money procured by the Presbytery of San Francisco with sizable funds from the Industrial Areas Foundation itself.

The assessment of achievements to date is part of the controversy. Detractors of the IAF point to the anti-Negro posture of Alinsky's first organizing efforts in Chicago, the powerful Back-of-the-Yards Neighborhood Council, organized in the late thirties on the ground of Upton Sinclair's book, *The Jungle*. This, say the doubters, is the fruit of amoral self-interest. Alinsky deplores the present racial resistance in Back-of-the-Yards, but points out that he believes in the genuine self-determination of neighborhoods, that he does not impose his personal goals on any organization which the IAF develops, and that he and the IAF have not been associated with Back-of-the-Yards for years.

The best-known effort of Alinsky has been in Woodlawn, the sprawling slum in Chicago which borders on the University of Chicago to the north. This is a nearly all-Negro community where the crises in black and white and dollars and cents are especially acute. Here the chronically unemployed, school dropouts, and a large percentage of welfare recipients add up to that peculiar mixture of apathy and hostility which is the heritage of the Negro in the worst neighborhoods of the ghetto. The Industrial Arts Foundation entered Woodlawn in 1960 at the invitation of several local clergymen. Much of the initial financial support came from the Roman Catholic archdiocese and the United Presbyterian Board of National Missions. Presbyterian involvement represented a co-operative effort between denominational units at the national and metropolitan level, and First Presbyterian Church in Woodlawn, a congregation older than the city itself. Under the leadership of copastors Charles Leber and Ulysses Blakely, the congregation decided to shape itself within the needs of the community in which it was located, and issued through its session the following statement:

Goals and Objectives of Our Christian Testimony in the Woodlawn Community and Larger Issues Related to the Needs of the Community:

    1. The Church must evangelize in this kind of community in a way which is consistent with the dynamics of this urban situation, not only in the traditionally individualistic way;

    2. The Church must take the initiative in the development of this area so that adequate standards and values for community life are established and maintained;

    3. The Church must avail itself of the opportunity for Roman Catholic and Protestant co-operation for community renewal;

4. The Church must support citizen participation in the planned redevelopment of a "disorganized" community;

5. The Church must support the development of independent and responsible Negro leadership in this urban Negro community;

6. There must be Protestant identification with legitimate Negro interest rather than the traditional identification with exploitive forces;

7. This organizational work must attempt to become part of a larger strategy for the breakdown of segregated patterns in the total Chicago metropolitan area;

8. The whole Church, clergy, local lay people, youth, etc., must be involved in the work of solving some of the critical problems of community life;

9. A strong enough organization must be developed to be able adequately to counteract the power of those interests which seek to continue to exploit segregated Negro neighborhoods;

10. As the Church participates in community life, it must acknowledge its own guilt for present practices and accept its particular responsibility to create, in the emerging new set of relationships, a delicate balance between love and justice.

Champions of the Industrial Areas Foundation point after five years to the following tangible achievements of the "Temporary Woodlawn Organization" set up by Alinsky's organizers—an organization which changed its name shortly after its inception, as a symbol of its sense of permanence and priority in the community, to "The Woodlawn Organization" (TWO):

1. Registration for voting of 2,000 people in a single day through a 46-bus cavalcade to city hall.

2. Twin program of tenant and landlord education through which many buildings have been repaired and improved.

3. Desegregation of a nearby beach (Rainbow Beach) in the summer of 1961.

4. City-wide influence in the struggle to obtain quality and integrated education in Chicago public schools, including the elimination of double shifts in ghetto schools.

5. Genuine citizen participation in urban renewal on the Woodlawn–University of Chicago "border" including a clear understanding that the University will not begin demolition for expansion until middle-income housing has been built to provide for relocated residents, and the joint sponsorship by T.W.O. and the Kate Maremont

Foundation of a 700-unit moderate-income project under 221D-3 of the Federal nonprofit housing program.

6. A contractual agreement between T.W.O. and the Department of Labor for the training of two hundred unemployed persons in the T.W.O. Job Retraining Program. This is especially significant because T.W.O. will be using indigenous leadership as well as setting policy for and supervising the professionals who are involved. Similar programs have foundered on the twin rocks of paternalism and welfare colonialism.[10]

To these positive claims the critics can respond, and do, that the misery and futility of slum living in Woodlawn has not been significantly altered in five years, that the picketing, mass meetings, and demonstrations that have characterized the TWO's program have split the church and the community and further alienated the very people who are in a position to really help the Negro achieve self-sufficiency.

Meanwhile, TWO became self-supporting at the beginning of 1966, no small achievement considering that the annual budget now to be raised within Woodlawn itself is between $30,000 and $40,000. The IAF, its organizing phase completed, is withdrawing, forcing the continuing organization to be self-sufficient and self-determinative.

Some Concluding Observations

1. A local congregation cannot participate in community organization, Alinsky version, without the backing of its denomination. There are several reasons for this. The most obvious is the expense. The local congregation "farther in" cannot guarantee the thousands of dollars Alinsky requires before he sends organizers into a community. In three years the Woodlawn organizations spent $177,500, of which only $27,000 was raised within Woodlawn. Other reasons are more subtle. No minister is going to plunge his congregation headlong into controversy without

[10] *Social Action* article, "If Justice Is the Goal, Organize" by Robert M. Davidson, Director, Department of Urban Church, Presbytery of Chicago, United Presbyterian Church, U.S.A., February 1965, pp. 9–11.

denominational sanction. Robert Christ in his report on the OSC, referred to earlier, makes this plain: "normal" congregational activities are suspended when organization begins, unsympathetic members leave, local congregational finances shrink, and the positive results that come from creative involvement of laity and clergy are delayed. Without denominational backing the local congregation is threatened with institutional suicide.

2. Local congregations have different roles to play in community organization. The role of the humanity-shaped congregation in the neighborhood organizing itself is evident. What about the congregation of the same denomination on the more affluent edge of the same city, the members of which may become the "enemy" when the IAF moves in? The role of the suburban congregation is like that of a parent who has to allow and even encourage his teen-ager to rebel and demand his freedom because there is no other way for the youth to achieve psychological power and ultimate social and economic independence. Although this comparison is fraught with its own kind of paternalism, it comes close to describing the necessary posture of the middle-class church member who must encourage the powerless to make demands on him, while, through his denominational coffers, he pays part of the bill.

3. There are other approaches to significant social change and the redistribution of power besides that embodied in the IAF. There is only one Alinsky; there are hundreds of ghettoes and poverty pockets in our major cities where the alienated live out their lives of desperation. Many of the forces and organizations working for social justice in the 1960's take the principles of conflict, power, and self-interest as seriously as Alinsky, the bid of the civil rights movement for political power being the most dramatic example. There are community organizations unaffiliated with the IAF which have achieved comparable although more modest and less publicized results; the program in a Midwestern city which forced the city to finish a long-delayed public housing project is one familiar to the writers. Alinsky has no copyright on the use of power to bring about change; rather he

is an eminently successful practitioner whose philosophy and methods need to be studied, applied, and when necessary altered and adapted to the specific situation. The issue- and structure-oriented ministries described in the following chapters are other approaches to some of the metropolitan crises to which the IAF addresses itself, and in their own way may ultimately make as significant contributions to a just social order.

CHAPTER 5

Issue-shaped Ministries

ON THE LINE

IT was a cold blustery day in early February. The scene: the front of a public elementary school in Cleveland, Ohio. On the sidewalk around the school a line of about two hundred people moved, carrying signs which read END SEGREGATION OF BUSSED PUPILS, FREEDOM NOW, DE FACTO SEGREGATION MUST GO. On the playground of the school, inside the circle of picketers, was another group of people, larger in number, more agitated in their actions. Shifting in and out of the picket line, and to and from the scattered clusters of people on the playground, were the reporters, cameramen, and radio-TV announcers.

In the picket line were a number of men wearing clerical collars. There were also housewives, business people, and students among the demonstrators. The marchers were obviously unaccustomed to their role. Some smiled, other wore frowns, and all stared straight ahead. No songs of freedom crossed their tight-clamped lips.

Individual members of the crowd pushed their faces into those of the demonstrators and spat on them. "You should be ashamed of yourself, Reverend!" "Go home, you don't live here!!" "Nigger-lovers!" Suddenly the crowd surged toward the marchers, forcing them into the busy street. One man in the crowd lifted high a sign he had snatched from the hands of a minister. The crowd laughed as the man with the sign tore it to pieces. Coffee in cardboard cups was passed out to the members

81

of the crowd. Curses aimed at the picketers tore through the air. Several belligerent bystanders stood talking to a jacketed man who held two vicious-looking dogs on short chains at the edge of the crowd and close to the picketers. A police car moved slowly past the school. It did not stop. The picketers kept marching.

Quality and Integrated Education

The situation that brought picketers and crowd to this place was a familiar one in the American city in the 1960's.[11] A school board had proven itself unwilling to face the issue of *de facto* segregation in the public schools of Cleveland. Previously the board had made arrangements to transport Negro pupils from overcrowded ghetto schools in the city to underpopulated schools in ethnic neighborhoods where Italians and Slovenians had long been the major nationality groups. Then the board had insisted on segregating the bussed-in pupils from students already in the school. Prior to the day of the picket line, both civil rights groups and residents of the neighborhood in which the school was located had met repeatedly with the Board of Education.

Civil rights advocates wanted the bussed-in pupils integrated into regular classes in the school. Neighborhood people wanted the bussed-in pupils removed from "their" school at once. Neither side received satisfaction. That February day marked the crossing of the Rubicon with respect to participation in the civil rights movement for many clergy and laity of the churches. The story of how clergy and laity became participants in this particular picket line goes back several months.

Facing Up to the Revolution

In 1963 the churches of America began to meet with new seriousness the injustices done to the Negro and the dynamic of

---

[11] The incident described took place at the William H. Brett Elementary School, Cleveland, Ohio. Similar events, having to do with *de facto* school segregation, transpired in virtually every major northern and western American city.

the civil rights revolution. The General Assembly of the United Presbyterian Church, U.S.A., meeting in Des Moines, Iowa, in May of that year set up a fund, one purpose of which was to aid in the establishment of offices and councils of religion and race in communities across the country. The first Office of Religion and Race established by the Presbyterians (even prior to the national Presbyterian Interboard Commission on Religion and Race) was in Cleveland. The Rev. Charles Rawlings, a man who had been in Cleveland for four years as director of the Presbyterian-operated Garden Valley Neighborhood House, was chosen to be its director. Rawlings had worked in the deep ghetto. He knew and was sympathetic with the plight of the Negro. With an initial budget of $20,000 provided by the Board of National Missions and the Presbytery of Cleveland, Rawlings began work in August 1963.

In the early months of its operation the Cleveland Office of Religion and Race was responsible for the initiation of scores of "dialogue groups" across the city. These had as their basis the experience gained the previous year when sixteen Presbyterian laymen met at Garden Valley Neighborhood House in an effort to understand the problems of life in the ghetto. In attempting to deal with the problem of the high rate of unemployment among Negroes, these particular laymen found that their own businesses engaged in subtle discriminatory hiring practices compounding the problems of the unskilled Negro in an automating economy. Subsequent to that disheartening discovery, they divided into two groups and began to meet with Negroes of backgrounds similar to their own, discussing the nature of the growing racial conflict in their city and the role they might play in its resolution. Each of the original two groups met five times, alternating between Negro and white homes. Before the meetings were over walls of prejudice began to tumble down and were replaced by bridges of understanding. Many in the two groups became deeply committed to the civil rights revolution.

With the experience gained prior to the creation of the Office of Religion and Race, Mr. Rawlings in his new capacity spurred the development of interracial "dialogue" groups across Cleveland. By early January, only six months after the Office of Religion and Race had been established, over eighteen hundred persons had participated in the discussion program, and a core of churchmen dedicated to racial justice had been identified.

From the outset the Cleveland Office of Religion and Race was ecumenical in nature. Although its director was responsible to the urban work director of Cleveland Presbytery for supervision and to the General Council of the Presbytery for policy guidance, an advisory board for the Office was quickly established which numbered among its members civil rights leaders, churchmen of other denominations, and university professors. The program never had a denominational focus.

The demonstrators on that crucial February day in 1964 were almost all alumni of the "dialogue" program. They had been brought together around the great issue of the day—racial justice. It is no exaggeration to say that, to a person, the picketers saw their march as a personal expression of their Christian concern.

In the days that followed, racial conflict in Cleveland swelled to the proportions of a major crisis.[12] There were picket lines, sit-in demonstrations, acts of civil disobedience, a political campaign, and a death. Through all these events the involvement of churchmen in the revolution in Cleveland deepened. Doctors and lawyers, teachers and housewives, clergy and salesmen, Negro and white were involved.

In April, in the midst of an act of civil disobedience directed at an intransigent Board of Education, the Rev. Bruce Klunder of the interdenominational Student Christian Union was crushed to death under the treads of a bulldozer. The city was stunned. The majority of the residents of Cleveland did not interpret Mr. Klunder's death as a sacrificial protest against racial injustice. Some even called it "Klunder's blunder." For the sympathetic, it

---

12 For a detailed commentary on the Cleveland racial crisis, the reader is referred to the *Cleveland Plain Dealer* and the *Cleveland Press* for the period January-May, 1964.

marked a second crucial turning point in the involvement of churchmen in the civil rights struggle.

For some weeks prior to the tragedy, a group of clergy had been meeting under the leadership of Charles Rawlings to exchange information on the racial situation in the city. On the morning following, almost two hundred of the clergy of metropolitan Cleveland, Protestant and Jewish, inner-city and suburban, met to form themselves into an Emergency Committee of Clergy for Civil Rights. An executive committee of seven was chosen to meet with newspaper publishers, public officials, and organized religious and welfare groups in the city to seek a way out of the educational impasse. The executive committee was given broad authority to formulate a strategy for expressing the concern of the religious community on the subject of civil rights.

In the following weeks Cleveland stumbled from crisis to crisis. The Emergency Committee became one of the best-known groups in the city. In late April it issued a call for the resignation of the entire Board of Education, which went unheeded. The pressure on the clergy was intense. Threatening phone calls, declining church offerings, and crucial confrontations between official boards and pastors were the order of the day.

Recognizing the need to harness the deep concern of the laity who had participated in the dialogue program, and other laity as well, an organization called Inter-Faith Laymen for Civil Rights established itself. Its members joined in the protests which were mounted around the subject of *de facto* school segregation.

In May a boycott of the public schools was called, which stands as one of the most successful school boycotts in the country. More than 90 per cent of all Negro pupils were out of school on boycott day. Dozens of freedom schools were held all over the city, staffed in large part by clergy and lay volunteers recruited through the Office of Religion and Race.

All these efforts were of little avail. Cleveland, perhaps to a degree unequaled in any major American city, refused to accept the challenge of quality, integrated education. The superintendent of schools resigned; the president of the Board of Education was replaced by another member of the board. Segregation deepened rather than declined. Three new schools were erected in the ghetto, which had the effect of resegregating even those pupils who had been bussed into predominantly white schools.

In the months that followed, the Emergency Committee of Clergy for Civil Rights continued to meet and to protest. A carefully prepared document entitled *Peace, Justice, and Public Education* was issued, which examined the quality of education offered in the ghetto schools and pleaded for a policy and program of desegregation by the Board of Education and the school administration. Conferences were held with the newly appointed superintendent of schools. Inter-Faith Laymen for Civil Rights also met. Its members fed into the established civil rights groups, CORE and the NAACP, and helped to man the scores of volunteer positions called for by the exigencies of the revolt.

Through it all, the Office of Religion and Race played a decisive role. The Emergency Committee of Clergy and the Inter-Faith Laymen were largely the result of Rawlings' leadership. From the beginning of the crisis his leadership, advice, and counsel were sought by the civil rights groups. He helped to recruit participants for picket lines and sit-ins. He was one of a group that organized and conducted the school boycott. In the presidential election of 1964 he helped promote a "march to the ballot box" in the ghetto. But his office was not only concerned with activist machinations. Through its director, the Office of Religion and Race stood by clergymen in trouble with their congregations for civil rights activities. The dialogue program continued and grew. Studies were published by the Office on *The Suburbanization of Cleveland's Negro Population, Race and Poverty*, and *Civil Disobedience*.[13] It initiated a major study of segregation in Cleveland schools, with grants from three of its supporting denominations. The research project utilized the serv-

[13] These studies were published in 1963 and 1964 by the Cleveland Office of Religion and Race, later incorporated into the Council of Churches of Christ of Greater Cleveland.

ices of a university professor and was intended to assist the attorneys involved in a NAACP suit on *de facto* segregation in the Cleveland public school system.

Almost a year after the Office of Religion and Race was organized, it had achieved genuinely ecumenical status. The Presbyterians relinquished their unilateral control, and five other denominations joined in its support: American Baptist, Disciples of Christ, the Episcopal Church, the Methodist Church, and the United Church of Christ, all through their local judicatories. During the first year of its existence Mr. Rawlings had made enemies among public officials, business leaders, and churchmen; and had made friends among Negroes, business and professional leaders, and churchmen. In spite of significant opposition within ecclesiastical ranks and the general community, the denominations now entered into an arrangement which assured that the witness and program of the Office would continue. Each denomination participating in the newly ecumenical Office of Religion and Race was invited to appoint two members to an administrative board to which the director was responsible. The denominational representatives on the board were supplemented by civil rights leaders.

Projects under way at the time of the transition to ecumenical support and control continued. The director developed a major leadership education program for Negro clergy and laity in co-operation with a local university. He mobilized support for some of the civil rights efforts in the South and helped Clevelanders to make their voices heard and presence felt in Washington.

Almost two years after the establishment of the Office of Religion and Race, Mr. Rawlings resigned to take a summer position with the Community Relations Service of the U.S. Government. The Cleveland denominations had previously decided to move the program concerns of the Office into the newly reorganized Cleveland Council of Churches, and he wished to give the denominational decision-makers a free hand in choosing staff for the new Commission of the Churches on Metropolitan Affairs (the department of the council slated to take over the "race" portfolio).

At the time Rawlings' resignation was announced, a letter appeared in one of the Cleveland daily papers, signed by a doctor and his wife. In part that letter read:

The old order changeth—or does it? There will no doubt be collective sighs of relief and even a few hollow cheers at the demise of the Office of Religion and Race as recently announced with the resignation of its director, the Rev. Charles W. Rawlings.

This represents not just the closing of another agency but the loss of a real ministry.

Besides the initiation of the interracial dialogue programs, organization of numerous laymen's groups, a center of meaningful communication during the tense atmosphere of last spring and summer, the Office of Religion and Race has provided in effect a "church" through which people of many faiths and races could work together to bring racial and social justice to Cleveland because they believed this work to be no less than the witness to which Christ called all men 2,000 years ago. Rev. Mr. Rawlings' ministry proclaimed this witness and provided the leadership through which others could express a similar commitment.

If this city, or any urban complex, is to survive the pressure of social upheaval produced by urbanization, good men of will in all churches must take the lead, and must act upon their conviction. Let us hope and pray that leadership of the Cleveland Council of Churches recognizes its responsibility to such churchmen. If this organization is too frail to live with controversy, organized religion will again fail to carry His message into the world.[14]

In the fall of 1965 Mr. Rawlings was hired by the Council of Churches as executive director of its Commission on Metropolitan Affairs. In spite of significant opposition within the congregations and the general community, the Protestant leadership were of one mind: Cleveland needed a forthright and militant posture on racial justice, and Rawlings was the man best qualified to deliver.

It would be dishonest to suggest that the cause of civil rights has been dramatically advanced by a Protestant office dedicated

[14] The *Cleveland Plain Dealer*, letter to the editor, by Dr. and Mrs. Frank Bruch, May 26, 1965, p. 12.

to racial justice. If it was unsuccessful in bringing about major changes in Cleveland, what were the contributions made by the Office of Religion and Race to the city and its churches?

1. Through the efforts of the director of the Office, hundreds of churchmen have been led beyond an academic interest in the struggle for racial equality to positions of genuine commitment. Before the Office existed many white Anglo-Saxon Protestants with enlightened private attitudes on matters racial were only too willing to sit quietly by and observe the struggles of the Negro. If questioned, they would admit a squirming discomfort at segregationist school policies, at discriminatory hiring and promotion policies, and at segregated housing patterns. But for the most part they refused to become involved personally. Through the personality of Mr. Rawlings, his uncompromising call to action, and his refusal to let go of an issue even when it led to community conflict, many churchmen in Cleveland have been brought to vigorous and dangerous involvement. The writers have been told by more than one, "I didn't think I could ever walk on a picket line, but here I am." They have heard clergymen testify repeatedly, "Rawlings led me further than I ever thought I could go in acting out my commitment to civil rights."

2. As a result of the ministry of the Office of Religion and Race, church members aggressively concerned for racial justice have identified one another. In individual congregations across the city, and across parish lines as well, people have met others who share their convictions and are willing to act. In most congregations of the major denominations in metropolitan Cleveland there are cadres of people who have shared the fear and exhilaration of the picket line, the numbing drudgery of addressing envelopes for a rally, or the exhausting effort of door-to-door solicitation for a voter registration campaign.

And something has happened to these people! As they talk about their participation in the fight for freedom, their faces glow with meaning and dedication. They speak with special fondness of those with whom they have shared the struggle. Clearly, they believe that the experiences provided through the Office of

Religion and Race are directly related to their Christian commitment and have made that commitment more real.

3. Many of the activities and programs of the Office of Religion and Race have a validity of their own. For example, the study carried out by the Office on *The Suburbanization of Cleveland's Negro Population* has been widely distributed among churchmen and public officials, businessmen and school administrators, social planners and suburban housewives. It is impossible to determine how metropolitan decisions have been affected by this and other studies prepared under the direction of the Office of Religion and Race. But these well-written and carefully documented studies have approached critical problems in the metropolis in an organized and intelligent way. This in itself has merit.

The same can be said of the leadership-education program for Negro clergy and laity undertaken by the Office in co-operation with Western Reserve University. In this program fifty key Negro clergy and twenty-five key Negro laymen were exposed to insights into the way their city operates and primed with suggestions for their own leadership roles within the community. Again, it may not be possible to point to specific alumni of this program who will function as outstanding leaders of the community in the days ahead. But some who participated will lead in significant ways; indeed, some have already done so.

4. The Office of Religion and Race has provided a line for the civil rights groups into the white churches. For many years, one of the problems which NAACP, CORE, and other civil rights groups have faced has been finding people to do jobs that need to be done. And churchmen have been frustrated by the perennial complexities of providing opportunity for significant service within the secular community. The Office of Religion and Race brought the needs of the civil rights groups together with the resources of the Church. Regular channels of communication were established between the Office and the denominations, so that when a need became apparent within the civil rights movement, Rawlings could place a half-dozen phone calls and know that key people were contacting those within their denomination who could deliver the necessary persons. One example may show the

effectiveness of the recruiting of volunteers. During a voter registration effort, an active participant in the structure and program of the Office of Religion and Race heard a civil rights leader bemoaning the scarcity of volunteer help. Two phone calls were made. Within twenty-four hours almost thirty volunteers—all churchmen—were on the streets of a ward in the deep ghetto, contacting unregistered residents. Such efforts may not produce immediate change in a large city, but the growing political power of the Negro, in which churchmen have had a hand, will ultimately bring about major overhaul in the life of the metropolis.

5. The Office has been responsible for helping the Church make a dynamic and consistent witness to the love ethic within the context of a concern for racial justice. In Cleveland, as in most cities, the churches and the clergy have been an arm of the "power order," placidly following the consensus as to what represents justice and progress. Only seldom and softly have the churches raised significant questions about the status quo. When Protestantism has agreed with anything like unanimity to tackle a problem, that problem has been usually related to the individualistic, pietistic ethic of Sunday closing, liquor laws, gambling, or pornography.

Before the existence of the Office of Religion and Race, churchmen in Cleveland were troubled by racial injustice, but their concerns were unfocused. Since its inception, the Office of Religion and Race and its director have provided direction and have forced churchmen to come to grips with the imperative to act on specifics. Since the February picket line, activist clergy and laity have frequently found themselves in a position of opposition to the organized business and political leadership of the city. During the height of the school controversy the Emergency Committee of Clergy for Civil Rights was attacked by major political figures; its statements were regularly scored in newspaper editorials. The leadership of the city sought peace; the Church—at least that part of it which shared the goals of the Office of Religion and Race—sought justice. Both goals are desirable. They are not always identical.

This has been a valid ministry. While it has not overtly assumed the traditional forms of proclamation, celebration, and pastoral care, each of these elements has been present in an unstructured and hidden way. The ministry has used and built upon the resources of the Church. Clergy and laity have been key components in the program of the Office. They have not been the only components; many who are irreligious or even anti-Christian have been involved in the activities of the Office. But always the Church, in the person of the director, the board, and the people who man the program, has been present.

The ministry has not been totally dependent on the charisma of the director, nor has it been the hobby of a self-appointed fellowship of concern. It was initiated by a denomination, financially supported by that denomination, and understood from the beginning to be part of that denomination's metropolitan strategy. Later, the Office of Religion and Race became an ecumenical activity involving six main-line denominations. Each of the senior executives of the local judicatories of these denominations came under some attack for having committed his denomination to the support of so controversial a ministry, but each withstood the attacks and provided support. Most recently it has become part of a denominationally structured and accountable council of churches.

The Need for Focus

A ministry for racial justice is a new departure. Along with subsequent religious and race projects in other cities and states, this ministry has singled out a specific issue and zeroed in. For years the Church has engaged in social action projects. The problem with this approach has been its broad and indeterminate nature. Analysis and pronouncement are not the same as specific actions aimed at achieving significant changes in power relationships, public policy, and patterns of group behavior. Intensive rather than extensive, particular rather than general, activist rather than reflective, this religion and race ministry has been vastly more effective than if it had been concerned with the entire spectrum of social problems.

A fantastic number of denominational and interdenominational race projects have come into being across the nation since 1963. A partial list of staffed officers or commissions at the metropolitan level would include by 1966 (there are dozens more unstaffed or part-time operations): the Greater Kansas City Council on Religion and Race, with George Laurent as executive director; the Detroit Commission on Religion and Race, with the Rev. Robert Hoppe as executive; the Chicago Commission on Religion and Race, with Robert Christ, executive; and, of course, the Cleveland Office.

Nor is race the only issue around which ministries of the Church have shaped themselves. In some metropolitan areas in the last half of the sixties, the Church has started to shape ministries around the issue of poverty and the Economic Opportunity Program. This, too, had led to conflict between the Church and established city leaders. In many communities, churchmen have sought to bring to pass metropolis-wide programs which are, in the words of the Economic Opportunity Act, "developed, conducted and administered with maximum feasible participation of residents of the areas and members of the groups served." New York, Chicago, Cleveland, and other cities have all had public officials who failed to take seriously the language of the Act or the church groups which pressed them to do so. Lois Willie, writing in the May, 1965 issue of *Renewal* quotes Chicago's Mayor Daley as having said, "When you say only poor people should have anything to do with running it, that's like . . . that would be like telling the fellow who cleans up to be the city editor of the newspaper."[15]

Nonetheless, poor people are intended by the Act to have a voice in the programs designed to break the chains of poverty, and clergy along with other concerned citizens have been pressing the matter vigorously. Clearly there is a role for the Church to play around the issue of poverty and the "war" that has been declared on it. The precise nature of the ministry to be developed

[15] *Renewal*, a publication of the Chicago City Missionary Society, May 19, 1965, p. 18.

around this issue is by no means clear. There is an organizational role: the organization of the poor in community action programs to change the status quo. There is a watchdog role: to see that "poverty" people and people from poor neighborhoods are represented in the decision-making bodies which approve and sometimes administer government-funded programs. There is a program role: such projects as "Operation Head Start" for preschool children and job training programs for teen-agers and young adults will inevitably involve Church organizations in some kind of partnership with the government. There is a prophetic role: welfare support needs to be augmented in every state and city by legislative action; the amount of money now being spent in our great cities is a temptation to corruption and waste; while the paternalistic and punitive way the poor are treated in American society needs to be denounced.

Meanwhile, the lessons learned from an issue-centered ministry such as the Office on Religion and Race apply equally to such issues as poverty. The ministry must be seen as a legitimate expression of Christian community. It must utilize the resources of the Church and be firmly based in a denominational or ecumenical agency. But it must deal with the secular world, its needs, challenges, and opportunities in its programming.

In the contemporary metropolis difficult issues will continue to thrust themselves at the Church. It is incumbent upon the Church, through association, diocese, and presbytery, to be willing to set apart men knowledgeable in the ways of the city and skilled in the social sciences to minister within the context of these issues, and to give them the freedom and support they need to do the job.

CHAPTER 6

Ministries to Structure

IN the two previous chapters, the reader has noted the struggles of the Church to move out into ministries that deal with the problems of the metropolis. Missionary monies, in previous generations of the Church expended in foreign lands and on direct services at home, are now being spent on controversial ministries clearly bent on changing the nature of our society.

This reflects more than a shift in the strategy of Evangelism. It also reflects a new seriousness on the part of clergy and laity, denominational leaders and theologians, concerning the ancient Judaeo-Christian idea that God is at work in His world. The Church has always said this officially, but has usually acted as though God's wondrous works were confined within institutional walls. The people of God have traditionally functioned as a kind of subculture, concerned for themselves, their structures, and their interpersonal fellowship. It is understandable that in this frame of reference is interpreted as the effort to get people *into* the Church.

The new seriousness with which the Church is taking the truth that God works in His world has meant that we are now beginning to be concerned about getting the people out of the Church and into the world. Perhaps the most significant contributions to this theological rapprochement between Church and world have come about as a result of the study of the World Council of Churches on *The Missionary Structure of the Congre-*

gation and the work of the task groups related to that study. To believe and to assert that God works out in His world, however, raises more questions than it answers. The church is then immediately faced with two significant problems:

1. Where and how is God at work in this world—especially the world of the metropolis?

2. In what way can the Church participate in His loving, redeeming, and creative work?

The seriousness of these questions is evident when it is recalled that the basic unit of organization in most churches of main-line Protestantism is and has been the residential parish. In earlier generations, when America was largely "small-town" or rural, the place of residence was the single most important fact that could be determined about a man. To locate the tangible and visible expression of the Church near his residence was sociologically sound. In the world of metropolis, however, as we have pointed out elsewhere, man no longer lives in so unitary a setting. Don Benedict's "worlds" of work, leisure, residence, and public sector underscore the fact that we all occupy multiple worlds. For the Church to focus its entire ministry upon the single world of residence, where a man may partake of a dozen meals a week, mow the lawn, and sleep, is both wasteful and irrelevant.

In the twentieth century man has organized himself into large and complex structures to accomplish the goals he sets for himself, his family, and his society. These organizations dominate virtually every area of life: education, manufacturing, government, charity, even leisure. To them, men from the universities, corporations, and government agencies give large parts of their time and loyalty. Yet within these structures the Church is not found, except as it is there in the lives of the men and women of the Church who work or play—who control or are controlled by these structures. Historically, the clergy have maintained that it is the task of the individual lay Christian to "carry" his faith and its implications into his work relationships, his public relationships, and his leisure-time activities. Few clergy, however, have understood the complexity of what they ask of their laity in this regard, especially in the interdependent, organized, corporate society of the contemporary American metropolis. The program, preaching, teaching, and organizational life of the residential congregation have simply not been planned or structured so as to permit the Church to be a staging area to prepare the laity for witness and ministry in the arenas where they normally operate.

Within recent years the denominations have begun to cooperate with one another in ministries that attempt to deal with the complex corporate structures of our society. These ministries are in their infancy and are few in number, but even their tentative existence throws light on the ways in which the Church must mount its mission in such a society as ours.

Among the oldest and most publicized of these structure-shaped ministries in America is the Detroit Industrial Mission. Founded in 1956 by the Rev. Hugh White, a priest of the Episcopal Church, the professional staff of the Mission now numbers five, with an annual budget in excess of $100,000 and the support of three major denominations. The Detroit Industrial Mission works on the premise that the major influence in a man's life is not his home but his work. Staff members make the point that the Church must be present in the business world if it is to have relevance in the twentieth century. Thus, the staff spend major portions of their time in the plants, the offices, and the union halls of the mammoth industrial complex which is Detroit.

In their work, the Detroit Industrial Mission staff do not seek to convert men to their own point of view or even to the Christian faith. They conceive their task primarily in terms of "presence"—i.e., the presence of the Church within the structure of industry and alongside the men who are part of the industrial scene. They are not "industrial chaplains" in the sense that they deal with the personal problems of an individual employee or a single member of management.

The Detroit Industrial Mission has antecedents in the worker-priest movement of postwar France and the Sheffield Industrial Mission in England. Both of these were efforts by segments of the

Church to understand the world of work and to be present in that world. Mr. White, while serving as rector of an Episcopal church in Ypsilanti, Michigan, observed the distance between the activities in his parish and the problems and concerns of his people in the postwar period. He realized that he, like other clergy, knew little of industrial life and that he was ill prepared to minister to the needs of his men who were part of that life. A period on the staff of the Parishfield Community, a Church training center outside Detroit, convinced him of the need to institute an industrial mission in Detroit. The support and encouragement of his denomination, at the outset embodied largely in Bishop Emrich of the Episcopal Diocese of Michigan, made it possible for the conviction to take shape in the Detroit Industrial Mission.

Staff time of the Mission is employed in four ways: in the shops and offices, in churches, in internal administration, and in research and writing. Each member of the staff is involved in all four of the various activities.

The nature of the work of the Mission in shops, offices, and union halls varies widely. In some shops, among hourly employees, it may take the form of simply participating in lunch-hour discussions and bull sessions. Here everything from production problems to presidential politics may be discussed. In other places, among other by-the-hour employees, the staff member may pursue a specially prepared curriculum dealing with the employee's relationship to the local union. Among management groups the focus may be on "ethics and decision-making"; or it may involve the presence of the Mission staff member in staff discussion on the varied problems of management. Sometimes the Mission may be present, through one of its staff, in a union bargaining committee. On at least some occasions, these bargaining committees have given major portions of time to the Mission in discussions of problems faced by the local union, the international, or even the union movement at large.

In no case is the posture of the Detroit Industrial Mission that of persuading, convincing, or lecturing. The technique used by the Mission among all industrial groups is the discussion-conference technique. The staff member may present a situation or a bit of background information to the group with which he is working. Then he questions and prods, aiding members of the group to develop their own understanding.

The Detroit Industrial Mission takes seriously its responsibility to work with established congregations and the denominations. Through publications, speeches, and conferences the staff makes available the insights it has gained to the clergy and laity of the churches. Sometimes vocational groups—e.g., salesmen—are gathered together in a residential parish to examine their own work in the light of their understanding of the Christian faith. On other occasions, men from several parishes and a number of occupations will be brought together to discuss the variety of problems present in their several vocations.

There is, it is clear, no groundswell within the churches of metropolitan Detroit to reorganize the programs of the hundreds of congregations in that area on the basis of the work of the Detroit Industrial Mission. Nevertheless, in the sympathetic and regular attention paid by the Mission staff to the ongoing life of the residential parish, a basis is being laid for a new theological understanding of what it means to say, "God is at work in the industrial world."

One of the lessons that has been learned in our corporate society is that any activity tends to become institutionalized, and its life tends to be expressed in institutional forms. This is true in the area of new ministries as elsewhere. Thus the Detroit Industrial Mission has administrative concerns and problems, and each member of the staff has administrative assignments. The staff meets together weekly for Bible study, theological reflection, and a discussion of their several activities. Once a year, members of the staff engage in a week-long retreat at which goals for the coming year are set. The Mission is governed by a board of directors comprised of fifteen members who represent the three supporting denominations as well as management and labor.

A quarterly newssheet is published entitled *Life and Work,* and monographs called *Occasional Papers* are issued from time to time. Recently, the staff changed from a time discipline—i.e., a given number of hours per week devoted to each project—to an objective discipline: i.e., the setting of particular goals and the achievement of those goals in a specified period of time.

Detroit Industrial Mission takes seriously its responsibility to think, study, and reflect. Each member of the staff has specific interests which he pursues in formal research. One, for example, is concerned with the change in the character of organized labor from "movement" to "institution." Another is studying the meaning of "participation" in a highly organized society such as ours, and especially within the industrial segment of that society. The papers that have resulted are among the more perceptive descriptions and proposals coming out of the Church's new ministries.[16]

Perhaps no more telling testimony can be given to the need for, and promise in, the industrial mission concept than this: the idea is spreading. At the date of this writing, industrial missions are to be found in Boston, Cincinnati, Chicago, Cicero, and Flint. Plans are under way for similar projects in numerous other industrial centers around the country.

All of this is not to suggest that the work of the Detroit Industrial Mission has proceeded without problems. In point of fact, one of the most serious problems of the Mission remains: how to get into the plants and offices of metropolitan Detroit. Management is often suspicious of the motives of the Mission, fearful that if they allow one such mission to be present within their corporate life others will seek to follow; anxious about whether staff members will seek to proselytize. The experience of the past has helped to allay some of these suspicions and fears, but doors still remain closed in the majority of plants in metropolitan Detroit.

One of the most serious problems faced by Detroit Industrial

[16] See, for example, "Mission to Metropolis," White & Batchelder, Detroit Industrial Mission, Occasional Paper No. 7.

Mission is that of retaining viable relationships with both management and labor in a city famous for its bitter struggles between these groups. There is a natural tendency for discussants to polarize around "management" or "union" points of view. Mission staff members have opinions and ideas regarding these disputes between labor and management. Nonetheless, the staff seeks to avoid becoming spokesmen for one or another of the management or labor attitudes that characterize so much of American industrial life.

It has been observed by some that because the Mission seeks to work *in* the plants, offices, and union halls, much of its freedom is compromised. Recently, for example, civil rights groups in Detroit threw a picket line around the central offices of one of the great corporations in that city, protesting alleged discriminatory hiring and promotion practices. While the Detroit Industrial Mission is strongly integrationist in its sympathies, staff members felt they could not participate in the picket line for fear of surrendering the confidence that some corporate officers had in them. Whether such a decision reflects real lack of freedom is for the reader to decide. The Mission makes good use of its in-plant contacts and relationships, and the strategic value for the mission of the Church of their on-site work must be weighed against the threat (or fact) of inhibited freedom.

The Detroit Industrial Mission has been in operation for a number of years, and while many of its conclusions and attitudes remain tentative, the staff vigorously rejects the idea that its work is experimental. "Through the Mission, the Church is present in industry. We intend to continue to be present—not for a while, but for a long while. We are not experimental." Thus one of the staff members commented to the writers in discussing his work.

When asked about the future, Detroit Industrial Mission does not have clear outlines of the ultimate direction of its work. The staff has, however, prepared a list of what they call "Proximate (Penultimate) Goals Induced from Industrial Life and Confirmed —in Our Opinion—by the Christian Faith."

Goals with Regard to Industry

1. To discover the meaning of the Christian gospel for the situation of men within the structures and institutions of industry and labor.

2. To discover ways of communicating the gospel in language and thought forms of men immersed in industry, business, and labor, in such a way that they may understand the meaning of the Christian message for their work situation.

3. To identify, encourage, and support men (Christian and non-Christian) in industry whose thought and action moves in directions consistent with the implications of Christian faith for industry as discovered in (1) above.

4. To influence structures and procedures of industrial organizations so that they will be more open to and encourage (rather than block and discourage) behavior and decisions contributing to the fullness of human life as understood by the Christian faith.

5. To discover and utilize in practice methods whereby men may support the fulfilling of human life, and resist the thwarting of human life, within their institutions.

Goals with Regard to the Church

1. Develop a form or instrument of the church that can bring the gospel and its meaning to the attention of men within the context of economic activity in modern industry—and can encourage their expression of Christian faith within the daily activity and decisions of corporate existence.

2. Develop, test, and document a discipline and a method for such an instrument of the church so that it can be duplicated by the church in other locations.

3. Influence the traditional forms and structures of the church so that in all its activities from parish church to the national level the church can be aware of and speak more relevantly to the new shape of society as brought about by industrialization.

Proximate (Penultimate) Goals Induced from Industrial Life
and Confirmed—in Our Opinion—by the Christian Faith

To encourage within the institutions of industry and labor:

1. Reflective thinking concerning long-range issues within industrial organizations.

2. Criticism and self-criticism leading to innovation and improvement within industrial organizations.

3. Improved dialogue-type communication vertically and horizontally within industrial organizations.

4. Responsible action reflecting respect for human beings at every level.

5. A broadening of the decision-making process to include as far as possible those affected by the decision, and to include information and questions relating to human welfare as well as production, profit, power, and a larger piece of the pie.

6. "Refusal to regard as final any enmity between persons and groups" (Horst Symanowski).

7. Openness to change and refusal to idolize what is.

8. Willingness to risk protest and to stand with those who are victims of unjust manipulation.

9. A contagious vision of industrial life "made for man."[17]

At the present time, in another part of the country, another ministry to the structures of metropolis is under way. Metropolitan Associates of Philadelphia is the result of an initiative of the American Baptists, but now enlists the support, either through staff or budget, of five denominations. Additional denominational involvement is anticipated as the program develops and matures.

Metropolitan Associates of Philadelphia is, in many ways, a more ambitious effort to minister to the structures of metropolis than is the Detroit Industrial Mission in that it takes as its target the entire structural complex of a vast metropolitan area. In a manner similar to the Detroit Mission, the Philadelphia project sees that existing congregations are residentially based and too often out of touch with the other worlds we inhabit. To minister to people in their complex worlds, there must be new attempts at involvement, understanding, and communication on the part of the Church. Unlike the Detroit Industrial Mission, Metropolitan Associates sees itself as frankly experimental, and discusses its methodology in terms of operational or action research. This phrase, when applied to staff, is defined in the following terms: "(1) They will pursue their mission within a research context guided and directed by research procedures, (2) in those defined

---

[17] From a mimeographed staff document of the Detroit Industrial Mission.

spheres and aspects of metropolitan life where the nature of missionary action is not clear, (3) by full time involvement in the secular structures on behalf of the church."[18]

The staff of Metropolitan Associates of Philadelphia is divided into three categories: lay associates, worker ministers, and urban agents.

The lay associates are theologically sensitive men and women from Philadelphia, chosen because of their deep involvement in Church and world. Already holding secular jobs at the time of their association with Metropolitan Associates, they bring a depth of understanding from long-time participation in and commitment to the structures of that particular metropolis. The context and nature of the employment of these lay associates ranges from sales management to city agency, from education to production in an industrial plant. It is anticipated that more than 100 lay associates will be involved in the near future.

The worker ministers take secular jobs in certain defined areas in order to discern from the vantage point of full involvement what it means to be obedient as a Christian in the world. Clergy are typically uninformed regarding the pressures, problems, and hopes of men and women in their work relationships. The involvement of the worker ministers is an effort to develop valid ministries, theologically based, within the context of the work world.

The urban agents may be either clergy or laity. They have been selected for their particular roles on the basis of the unusual skills and qualities each possesses. They do not hold secular employment; rather, each is assigned to a specific slice of metropolitan life. Within that slice, in a manner similar to a reporter or a social researcher, the urban agent is to be where the action is. It is anticipated that the free-wheeling nature of the assignment, coupled with the skills and qualities the urban agents

[18] From a mimeographed document entitled "Metropolitan Associates of Philadelphia," seventh draft, p. 5.

possess, will enable them to acquire understanding, to participate in the process of social change, and to communicate the nature of change to the Church and its institutions. Urban agents are active in the following functional sectors of the city: arts and education, biological and mental health, social organization, politics and government, business and industry, and physical developments.

The key to an understanding of the Philadelphia project is the concept of involvement in social change. Through its own involvement, Metropolitan Associates seeks to be a responsible interpreter of the events which occur within the metropolis, and an agent by which man is called to responsible action within the metropolis. The project will be financed in the following manner: (1) the worker-ministers will earn their own salaries in secular employment, but maintenance expenses while job-hunting, as well as moving expenses and pension dues, will be assumed by the budget of the project; (2) the lay staff will earn their own salaries; (3) the urban agents will be supported by their own denominations through the Metropolitan Associates program. The board of managers of the project consists of two representatives of each of the co-operating denominations, plus five selected at large. The Metropolitan Associates of Philadelphia co-operates with the Philadelphia task group of the "Missionary Structure of the Congregation" study, which serves as its advisory committee. This liaison relates the project to the National Council of Churches and the World Council of Churches, but it is an independent entity.

The reader may object at this point, "The Church has long been involved in society's structures, especially through the social action offices of the various denominations." There is obviously truth to such a statement. For instance, for many years organized Protestantism has attempted to bring its ethical insights to bear on society through the structures of government. Even the most casual review of history brings to mind the temperance movement, woman's suffrage, gambling, and civil rights. Here are areas in which the influence of the Church on legislative matters has been significant. What differs now, in the efforts of the Church to deal with the structures of society, is the style.

Historically, the Church in its work of social action has exerted an "influencing" role. This approach has almost said, "The Church stands apart from the structures of society. We reserve the right to judge and to attempt to change, but we are not really part of this world." Let it be quickly admitted that his analysis cannot be pressed too far. Many social action figures, Church lobbyists, have lived in Washington and have come to know as friends both legislators and governmental staff members. Nonetheless, the basic position the Church has assumed in its relationship to government has been on the outside. It will readily be seen that this involves a substantial difference from these newer ministries within the industrial structure, where the staff member leaves the world of the residential church and casts his lot, as a confessor of Christ, wholly on the structure within which he serves. In the case of eight of the clergy in the Metropolitan Associates of Philadelphia, even Church support is relinquished for the support to be earned in secular employment.

This different approach to ministry within structure seems to be having its effect on the social action people in Washington and New York. More and more, the writers believe, those who represent their denominations at the seats of governmental power are taking on some of the presuppositions to be found in the work of Detroit Industrial Mission and the Metropolitan Associates program. (Some of these social action leaders may argue, on the contrary, that these latter-day organizations have been influenced by *their* work and changing philosophy.) In a letter to the writers, one of the denominational men in the nation's capital commented on his work in the following way:

Ninety per cent of it is cultivating and enlarging personal contacts with governmental and non-governmental people who are close to the places where program and policy is developed in the areas of civil rights, civil liberties, and church-state relations. Out of these contacts and the numerous meetings that are connected with them, is supposed to come the insight and knowledge that will enable the Washington office to act responsibly and intelligently as a "policy counselling" agent to the judicatories and boards of the Church. At the same time, one hopes that there is some flow the other way in these various conversations and meetings, so that the church contributes in both an informal and a formal way (e.g., in formal testimony before various committees), though in very limited degree to be sure, to the process of program and policy formation.

While the arena differs substantially from those in which other structure-shaped ministries work, the language, the unstated presuppositions, and the goals of this "lobbyist" for the Church remain similar to those felt and articulated in the newer ministries.

ATTUNED TO OTHER WORLDS

Protestant Christianity is taking more and more seriously the responsibility to work and become knowledgeable in the "other worlds" man inhabits. This work takes place on the basis of the following assumptions: that God is at work in the world; that it is the responsibility of the Church to point to those places where God is at work and to join Him in His work; that the Church is ill prepared at the present time, given its almost exclusive residential base, to know where God may be at work in the world.

These assumptions have led the new ministries in structures to stress "presence" in the nonresidential world. Until recently, preachers and theologians spoke of the brokenness, the anonymity, and the turmoil of the metropolis to the exclusion of almost any other insights into urban culture. Today, in a new spirit of humility, the Church is beginning to confess that it has much to learn from the world of strip cities, suburbs, cybernetics, and satellites that is positive and good. The Church is moving out, tenuously, into the structures man has built, in which it is recognizing with fresh insight that God is at work. It is standing alongside the production worker and the manager, the public official and the educator, the scientist and the artist. To be sure, the Church feels strange in these surroundings: naked, shorn of the glib responses in which it has clothed itself. But it stands, and in its stance the Church encounters the God of men and events.

CHAPTER 7

Dialogue Ministries

THE Church, through its newer ministries, has committed itself in recent years to at least three levels of involvement in the world outside the residential parish. The first of these levels—conflict—is exemplified by the participation in community organization and in issue-shaped ministries. The second level, that of influence, is one which has a longer history in the life of the denominations as they have related to government. Influence is also present to some degree in the newer issue-shaped ministries. The third level of Church involvement in the world—namely, presence—is to be seen in ministries within structures, and is perhaps best exemplified by the Detroit Industrial Mission.

Significantly, each of these forms of ministry is concerned with man in his corporate context. While these ministries have been developing, another style of service has been growing up, running along a quite different track. This ministry—which we have designated as dialogue ministry—stresses the importance of the single person, is usually expressed in one-to-one relationships, and takes place in the leisure and recreation sector of the society.

There is more to the life of the metropolis than loneliness, brokenness, and anonymity, elements which theologians and preachers are fond of decrying. Vocational opportunity, cultural advantage, and personal fulfillment are also facts of our urban situation. But it must not be forgotten that there are many within the city who are desperately lonely, who feel themselves out of touch with the world that rushes by them and at the same time engulfs them. Out of the recognition that there are some who do not easily find their places or develop a satisfying set of relationships—and find a faith that sings—the Church in recent years has put financial and human resources into ministries designed to provide the context in which meaning and relationship may be found through dialogue.

Who are the lonely and out-of-step on the metropolitan scene? Why have they found themselves out of communication with the dynamic life of the city? To deal with either of these questions extensively would take several books and a mastery of technical disciplines beyond the scope of the authors' competence. It is, however, possible to sketch some answers. Our society is family-centered. We assume that people will marry, work from nine to five, and have children. Ours is a society which expects and even demands certain kinds of conformity: a man works at a "respectable" job, he wears a certain cut of clothes, and he lives in a house where the green grass grows all around. Those who do not fit comfortably into these patterns, set by an informal but decisive American consensus, are effectively beached beside the stream of contemporary life.

The young person has few places where he can express his own unique identity. He is forced to go to school, and there he must abide by the rules and patterns imposed by the educational system. He must fulfill certain demands his family makes of him. He is obliged to participate in structures which he has not made, and which he might not choose were he free. The high-school and college young person is in an age group in which disaffection from society has been the rule for centuries, and there is a sense in which he discovers his identity in the expression of this disaffection.

Like the adolescent, the single young adult is outside the accepted pattern and even more than the adolescent tends to be forgotten by society. If he is young and single, his married friends have their own lives to lead, and they take for granted that he is caught up in the ritual of courtship and will soon be married himself. If he is past thirty and single, people tend to be suspicious of his sexual proclivities. If he is widowed or divorced, he has learned a pattern of life within a family structure that now is denied him. The Y's, the churches, and other membership organizations carry on activities and programs that assume a family identity among their members.

Likewise the creative person, or the one seeking to discover whether he is, in fact, capable of producing significant art, often finds himself looking at rather than swimming in the main currents of American life. His observations of the city, its people, its values, and its style may be intensely critical. Therefore he is not accepted by, nor does he wish to accept, those who are comfortably settled into the style of life of the American city. His creative work is probably pursued in a solitary setting, but he needs the impact on his life of others who share the rejection of society and the struggle to portray the quality of contemporary existence in creative art forms.

As the Church has attempted to enter into dialogue with the people of metropolis, the artist, the young adult, and the youth are those for whom this special ministry has relevance, and among whom it has found the greatest appeal.

The locale in which dialogue ministry has most often taken place has been the coffeehouse, but this has not been the only expression of it. There are dialogue ministries centered in suburban shopping centers; one such is outside of Baltimore, Maryland. There is a dialogue-type ministry on the slopes of one of our western ski resorts. There is a night ministry in San Francisco, centering on the bus depot, the bars, and the street corners. There are a handful of unattached ministers who walk the streets of some of our large cities, entering into discussion and conversation with whomever they meet. There is a dialogue-type ministry in a Las Vegas luxury hotel, where the minister works as a desk clerk eight hours a day, and during his off hours serves those whom he meets through his work. Dialogue ministries come in a wide assortment, and it seems safe to assume they will take still other and perhaps more unusual forms, but since the coffeehouse is clearly the most popular of these ministries let us examine one with some care.

As you enter the coffeehouse, any time after ten o'clock in the evening, a variety of sights and sounds assail you immediately:

The people. There are some who are obviously "just looking," quietly drinking their coffee, smoking cigarettes, and noting carefully the events that unfold before their eyes. By contrast, there is a larger number for whom this is a second home, maybe even their only real one. They are bent over the tables in earnest, laugh-punctuated conversation with their companions. A few sit on the floor, their legs drawn under them so people can pass without stumbling, their demeanor casual and cool. Informally clothed, several men are bearded and a few of the women wear their hair long and straight to the shoulders. If there is affectation in these departures from the conventional norms of dress, an air of revolt in clothing and general appearance, it is equally obvious that these people are comfortable in this place.

Physical appearance of the coffeehouse. It looks markedly different from a commercial restaurant. The room is small and usually hot. The pictures that line the walls are not ones you would find in a Howard Johnson's restaurant. Instead they are serious artistic efforts, twisting, slashing kaleidoscopes of color and form. The lights are low, the soft glow of a living room rather than the blackout of a posh cocktail lounge. No cash register jangles its commercial rhapsody; no costumed waitresses serve the tables.

The sounds. Conversation is animated and intense much of the time. Laughter, wisecracks, and jokes are tossed between tables. Then the talk dies down and it is concert-hall quiet while a giant in blue jeans plays a guitar and sings. The lilt of a folk song or a song of the civil rights revolution fills the room. Everybody joins in the chorus. A poet stands up and reads an original indictment of the idiocy of contemporary folkways, and when he finishes, his subject and technique quickly become the topic of conversation at the tables. The offerings of singer and poet are not of professional quality. There is more gravel in the voice of the singer, there are more self-conscious shock words and values in the poem. But the mood of both is one of earnestness rather than polish, of intensity rather than slickness. As the young nonhero, Holden Caulfield, of *Catcher in the Rye* might put it, "There is nothing 'phony' about their performance."

Perhaps the most singular aspect of the coffeehouse goes unnoticed at first. No one goes it alone. Everyone is sitting with someone. Each person is related. Those who come in alone are quickly joined by people already in the room. This is true unless a loner makes it clear at the outset that he wishes to sit in solitude. Even then, later efforts may be made to establish a relationship.

There is human warmth, an honest kind of openness, and genuine interpersonal involvement in a coffeehouse operated under the auspices of the Church. But in many ways, even to the careful observer, an evening in a "Christian coffeehouse" is similar to one in any one of dozens of commercial establishments sprinkled all over the nation. In what respect is a Christian coffeehouse different?

What's the Difference?

In the first place, the motivation is different. In a Church-sponsored coffeehouse the goal is not to make money or even to meet expenses. Virtually all these operations are heavily subsidized; most have financial problems in maintaining a sufficiently sound financial base to continue in business. The motive is to reach out to people on behalf of the Church, to help people relate to one another in a fellowship deeper than the glad hand, and to provide a context within which honest confrontation, discussion, and acceptance can take place. The conditions of urban life make it difficult for these experiences to happen by chance, and the Church, through its involvement in dialogue ministry, acts as an enabler.

Second, a Christian coffeehouse is different from a commercial venture because it involves a committed group of people who, beyond manning the coffeepots, are trained to initiate discussions, draw people out of their self-conscious in-dwelling, and express their own faith in the conversations which ensue. One coffee-house with which the writers are familiar calls its waiter-partici-pants "servants." For several months prior to the opening of this particular ministry, the servants studied books together, exposed to one another the deeply personal dimensions of their own faith, splashed paint on walls, and built tables and benches for the store they had rented for their venture. When the coffeehouse opened each agreed to serve for a given period of hours each week. This particular servant group continues to meet together for two hours a week. They study the Bible and books of theology; they share their experiences in the coffeehouse, they discuss problems that have arisen and develop policy for the ministry.

A third difference between the commercial and the Christian coffeehouse is this: in the house committed to ministry, decisions regarding procedure are made by a board consisting of the waiter-participants and those who are part of the life of the establishment. In practice this has usually meant that Christian ministry has been the presupposition on which policy decisions are made. Pressures such as meeting expenses or weeding out "undesirables," which might become the basis for decisions in a program for profit, are measured against the concern for witness and service.

Who's with the In-Crowd

There are problems in dialogue ministry. Some of them are severe enough to bring into question the entire concept. One of the most severe has to do with the coffeehouse becoming a hang-out for small, tightly knit in-crowds. Faced with this kind of crisis, the waiter-participant must maintain an emphasis on per-sons rather than groups, seeing that all the loners are drawn into discussion and encounter. In at least one coffeehouse the police of the city have raised anxious questions because a group of dissident young people have made it their regular meeting place. The servant group at the house, in concert with the business manager, have succeeded in treating each gang member as an individual—have not given special privileges to the gang, have welcomed strangers and the solitary, and have been able to save the house from being identified with a particular group.

In another coffeehouse, where most of those who come are in the under-twenty-one age bracket, two nights a week have been reserved for people over twenty-one. On these two nights the servant group has noticed a growing attendance of parents of the teen-agers who frequent the place on other nights. Parental participation has been encouraged in order to help parents understand the milieu in which their youngsters congregate during leisure hours.

Another problem of the coffeehouse ministry is more theological in nature. The nonconformist, open-ended posture of the place often appeals to individuals who are nonreligious or even hostile to religion. In this kind of permissive environment the waiter-participants are often at a loss to know the precise moment when they can share the specifics of their Christian convictions and beliefs. Not one of them wishes to convey the impression that the coffeehouse is simply a covert means of preaching to or at those who come. Nevertheless, they are convinced that their faith is relevant to the topics under discussion and should be brought to bear on them.

This problem of encounter between the committed and the religious outsider has another puzzling aspect. In the case of responsible adults who feel drawn to a supportive relationship with the coffeehouse—who are excited about the opportunities it affords for personal encounter and growth, but are by their own admission outside the Christian camp—this question arises: Is there a place for these people in the servant group? Sharing many of the concerns of the group, they still do not bring an explicitly Christian motivation. There is no easy answer to this question, which really exposes the tension between the universality and particularity of the Gospel.

There are so many dialogue ministries operating under Church auspices across the country that it would be impossible to enumerate them all. It would be equally impossible to describe with accuracy the manner in which they are governed and financed. Variety is the rule: some are operated by individual congregations, others by local judicatories of denominations, some by intercongregational groups, some by denominational boards of home missions. Financing may come from churches, denominations, individuals, special offerings; most utilize all these resources as available.

Whatever their financial undergirding, Church coffeehouses have been named with both vigor and humor. They are called: The Precarious Vision, The Loft, The Jawbone, The Well, The Goblet, Encounter, The Potter's House, and so on. They thrive in large cities—New York, Chicago, San Francisco; and in very small cities—Burlington, Vermont; Lancaster, Pennsylvania; Vermilion, Ohio.[19]

In the fall of 1964 one of the more ambitious dialogue ministries was launched in San Francisco. Given the name "Intersection," this ministry set out to relate the arts, the Church, and the community in a vital way. Intersection and its director, the Rev. O'Linn McGuire, Jr., initiated the program in the rear of The Precarious Vision Coffeehouse. Almost immediately after opening he began planning an ambitious series of exhibits, performances, seminars, and discussions.

In a mimeographed document explaining its purpose, Intersection is called "an experiment which is attempting to demonstrate how the Church can find a more relevant ministry by utilizing the creative arts and involving both itself and the community of which it is a part." In 1965 Intersection moved from its original and temporary quarters (The Precarious Vision had, in the meantime, voluntarily disbanded its board of directors and come under the auspices of Intersection) to a newly refurbished facility on O'Farrell Street. New facilities include a coffeehouse,

[19] For a more extensive listing of coffeehouses and practical suggestions for staffing, operating, and funding a coffeehouse, see "The Church Coffee-House," a mimeographed guide prepared by John P. Peck, Department of Church Planning and Research, Protestant Council of the City of New York.

a theater, an arena, a gallery, and office space. As program has developed, Intersection has provided for the presentation and discussion of creative drama and programs in the visual arts (including films and the dance), music, and literature.

Intersection is currently supported by the Methodists, the United Presbyterians, and the United Church of Christ. Additional funds come from the Glide Foundation, the YMCA, individual patrons, and coffeehouse income. A board of directors selected from supporting agencies in the community at large is charged with initiating policy, managing funds, approving program, and selecting staff. Present staff includes a director, secretary, janitor, coffeehouse manager, and a seminary intern. Future plans include retaining a theater director and gallery manager.

There is now sufficient experience in dialogue ministry to permit a measure of generalization: First, the "teaching" ministry that takes place within the context of dialogue is essentially undogmatic in nature. Doctrinal statements are not offered as answers to those who ask questions. Explicit statements of faith are usually preceded by a nonargumentative, "This is what I believe." And yet it is obvious to all who serve and who come that the motivation of the coffeehouse is grounded in the Christian faith, and that the waiter-participants are engaged in a servant discipline related to this Christian faith. In point of fact, very much as the Detroit Industrial Mission sees its role as presence in the industrial world, so the dialogue ministry sees its role as presence in the name and spirit of Christ with persons.

Second, the quality of commitment of the waiter-participants —the servant group—is crucial in developing a significant ministry. In virtually all the dialogue ministries, including other than coffeehouse ministries, there is a supportive lay group that works with the clergyman. In some ministries no ordained clergyman is even present. The entire program is directed by the laity of the Church. Servants must develop a group identity, must understand the purposes of the ministry, and must be so informed and secure regarding their own faith that they can express it with confidence even in face of attack. A period of training, an explicit discipline, and a continuing group life are necessary if the servants are to minister effectively.

Third, in a majority of the dialogue ministries there is a concern for art and the artist. The Church has seldom known how to relate to the artist, even when it has tried. Sometimes it has ignored him, sometimes censured him; sometimes it has tried to use him—and only too often has alienated him. In the person-centered ministry as exemplified in the coffeehouse, the Church has had moderate success in establishing common cause with poets, painters, and those who make music. Many of the themes with which contemporary art wrestles—the fractured quality of life, the quest for meaning, the struggle for self-understanding —recur again and again in the dialogue ministries. This is why coffeehouse walls are literally papered with paintings and etchings; this is why the performers act out, sing, or read their works. If the creative artist is one who sees real value in the person for his own sake, it is natural and right that the Church as it ministers to the person should lock arms with the artist.

Finally, and most important, it is clear that genuine community and commitment can develop through dialogue ministry. People do care about others they have come to know through discussion and argument; people with whom they have shared artistic and aesthetic pleasures. In the dialogue ministry reconciliation across racial lines, between age groups, and among economic and social levels has occurred. There are moments akin to worship as the group celebrates the sacrament of life. One young adult finds absolution and acceptance through informal confession at the coffee table; another individual struggles through doubt to a faith that works. Because dialogue ministries in the world of leisure create the climate in which experiences like these can happen, the ministry is amply justified. Indeed, the achievements of dialogue ministries point to the need for expanded ministries in recreational and resort areas, and the need for more intensive outreach to groups that coffeehouse and other current programs miss, namely, the older adults, both single and married.

PART IV

Ecumenical Explorations in Metropolis

Archbishop William Temple thirty years ago referred to the ecumenical movement as "the great new fact of our age." A wide variety of current authors have, explicitly or by indirection, referred to urbanization as the great fact of our age. How do these two observations, reflecting two different windows on the world in which we live and move, relate to one another?

There is a growing recognition among the leaders of Protestantism that a relevant ministry to the cities, which have become the basic context of contemporary existence, can only be realized as the denominational families stand together in mission. As a consequence of this insight, a diversity of ecumenical ministries is now to be found in every American metropolis of any size. In this section, attention will be given to councils of churches, group ministries, and chaplaincies, three significant expressions of the ecumenical impulse.

CHAPTER 8

Service or Servanthood

THE impulse to Christian unity has always been strong within the body of Christ. In the early centuries of the Church this incentive was realized through the great ecumenical councils, the struggles to develop a systematized and integrated theology, and loyalty to the successors to the apostles: the patriarchs in such great metropolitan sees as Antioch and Constantinople. In the Middle Ages Western Christendom, with the papacy and the scheme of life that embraced sovereign, knight, and serf, insured a considerable degree of organizational unity. Although the Reformation sundered the organic unity of the Western Church, two kinds of unity may be seen in the post-Reformation period: one, encompassing the Catholic tradition, emphasizing loyalty to the pope as the base of oneness; the other, encompassing the churches of the Reformation, emphasizing the authority of the Scriptures.

In America in the eighteenth, nineteenth, and early twentieth centuries the proliferation and intensification of denominationalism made the impulse to unity an ideal rather than a fact. Nonetheless, in the nineteenth century numerous movements evolved which had as their goal the actualization of the one Body of Christ. Notable among them were the Disciples of Christ, who grew out of the concern for unity felt by Alexander Campbell and Barton Stone. The paradoxical result of their concern was its culmination in still another denominational family.

Every movement to give organic expression to the unity of the Body of Christ did not result in a new and separate structure. In the early nineteenth century another movement began under the aegis of the impulse to unity, a movement which has affected the course of Protestant Christianity to this day. That movement has been most accurately described as co-operative Christianity and has had its institutional expression largely in councils of churches.

Co-operative Christianity as a distinct movement was really initiated by Sunday-school workers. In 1832, 1833, 1859, and 1869, conventions of Sunday-school workers drawn from many denominations were held in the eastern United States. Laymen and clergy at these conventions discovered common concerns as they discussed how to teach children the content of the Bible and the nature of the Christian faith. In 1872 Protestant churchmen in America agreed to a uniform series of Sunday-school lessons for their churches.

During these same years and into the early twentieth century a level of co-operation was developing on the far-flung mission fields of Protestantism which reflected a commitment to the fundamental unity of the Church of Christ. "Comity," the designation of geographic areas where a particular denomination may operate without competition from its counterparts, was first spelled out on the foreign missions field. Today this concept is known and accepted in the American city, especially in the establishment of new residential congregations in the suburbs. Foreign missionaries were first to recognize the need for interdenominational co-operation, and the folly of replicating, in foreign lands, the institutional overlap of American denominationalism.

By the closing decades of the nineteenth century the ancient impulse to unity had become institutionalized in Church federations, organizations which embodied unity through programs that included interdenominational worship, lecture programs, training for Sunday-school teachers, and occasions of fellowship for men, women, and clergy of co-operative churches. By

the second decade of the twentieth century the federation movement was in the ascendancy, although only a few federations
had paid staff at that time. From the period of World War I to
the present day, the movement for co-operative Christianity has
proliferated councils of churches and church federations. They
are to be found in virtually every American city of any size, in
every state in the union, and at national and international levels
as well.

Congregations and Their Councils

Metropolitan councils, with but few exceptions, are organized
on the basis of the local church. That is, local congregations are
the constituent bodies of the metropolitan council of churches.
Money is set aside in local church budgets to help finance the
work of co-operative Christianity; members of local churches,
representing themselves or their individual parish and not the
denomination of which they are a part, sit on the governing
boards. The local council of churches tends to be an umbrella
organization under which may be found most of the churches
of the main-line denominations in the city in question.

The congregational basis of the local council of churches
accounts for the program of the council. There are generally two
categories of program: activities that serve the local churches,
and those that provide direct services to people. Thus a typical
metropolitan council of churches will include a program in
Christian education, the primary thrusts of which are teacher
education for Sunday-school teachers and a co-operative youth
organization usually designated as a United Christian Youth
Fellowship. The local council may have a radio and television
department which will appropriate a share of the public affairs
time of local stations in the name of co-operative Christianity.
A council may have a department of social welfare concerned
for the distribution of food and clothes to the needy, the oversight of chaplaincy service in homes for the delinquent or jails,
and the development of a Protestant voice among social work

agencies and professionals. The local council of churches may have auxiliaries for Church men and women (usually separately) which sponsor tours, promote informational programs, and encourage the adoption of "service" projects. In addition, there may be a department on Church extension to deal with comity arrangements, a department on music which strives to enhance the caliber of Church music in the city, and a department on audio-visual aids which provides equipment to local churches and their staffs. Almost certainly there will be a united ministerial fellowship which encourages fellowship and discussion of common concerns among the clergy of the various denominations in the city.

The staff of the local council of churches will reflect its program of service to the churches and direct service to people. A "typical" council of churches will include on its staff an executive director, a director of Christian education, and staff people in the areas of social welfare, research, television and radio, music, or some combination of these. For the local church the council staff provides a ready source of pulpit supplies, program speakers, and resource guidance.

It is common to hear people say, when describing their commitment to the council of churches, "We do together the things we cannot do alone." This statement usually means that the council of churches staff becomes affiliate staff of the local churches; the council programs become supplementary programs to local churches.

Councils of churches are notoriously underfinanced. Few of them function without recurring crises in meeting the payroll, paying the rent, and funding programs. W. P. Buckwalter, Jr., has indicated that the five primary sources of income for metropolitan councils are local church budgets, individuals, community chests, offerings taken at co-operative programs or services, and program fees.[1] In at least two large American cities, New

---

[1] W. P. Buckwalter, Jr., in *Growing Together, A Manual for Councils of Churches,* from the chapter "Finance" (New York: the National Council of Churches of Christ in the U.S.A., 1955), pp. 96–109.

York and Chicago, council financing is partly cared for by fifty-
or hundred-dollar-a-plate dinners to which leading industrialists
and professional men are invited. At these dinners additional
pledges of support for the council program are received.

As previously indicated, the local council of churches is typically governed by a board of directors made up of selected
representatives from local churches. These board members will
include business leaders, professional men, clergy (usually of
large suburban churches, but often from among those who
serve smaller churches, yet have a real ecumenical passion), and
a few denominational executives or leaders. The board of directors may be quite large in some councils of churches, and is
often supplemented by an executive board to whose hands are
entrusted the real operating decisions.

The captivity of the conciliar movement within the scheme of
the residential parish has meant, almost without exception, that
the metropolitan council has been a "tame animal." The local
church principle of organization means dozens of "bosses," all
of whom must be served, placated, and regularly solicited for
funds. From time to time councils have sought to take militant
stands on issues, mobilize the moral impact of the churches, pro-
nounce judgment on social evil, and create dramatic new ministries. But when this has been done the staff is called to task
around the issue of its "right" to speak and act for Protestantism.
The structural divorce from denominational decision-makers has
made their sanction in controversial matters difficult to obtain;
the bold council finds itself out on a limb, its legitimacy suspect
and its sources of supply threatened by displeased trustees in
local congregations.

Because of the conservative and cumbersome mold into which
the council that is accountable to local congregations has been
forced, churchmen with a passion for justice or a commitment
to experimental ministries have felt impelled to set up agencies
which cross denominational lines but are not under the aegis
of the council of churches. Thus, may American cities have been
faced in recent years with a multiplicity of Protestant images:

one projected by the council of churches and others by newer agencies, such as the ministries to issues and structures described earlier in these pages. Yet the power implicit within the Protestant community, and the impact that such power might have on the metropolis, is considerable indeed. Could not local councils of churches be organized and structured so as to serve and change the metropolis? The issue is self-service or servanthood. Are Protestant churches and churchmen content to have their co-operative witness limited to serving and pleasing the institutional needs of local congregations, or can they unleash their potential power for genuine servanthood out in the world in which the Lord of the Church has set them?

THE IMPERATIVE TO RESTRUCTURE

In the years since World War II a multiplicity of problems have been thrust into the consciousness of the American people. The cold war, McCarthyism, the civil rights revolution, the blight in the American city, and poverty have all drawn major attention and the interest of large sections of the American public. These same years have seen a growing recognition by the Church that it can and must address itself to the problems of a growing urban culture. What is more important, churchmen have recognized in growing numbers that actions to alleviate the suffering present in such a culture must accompany the brave words that sound forth from pulpit and denominational gathering. In another perspective, the years since World War II have been years in which Church leadership, at least as represented by the major Protestant denominations, has recognized that individual piety is inadequate as the primary expression of Christian commitment, and that pure congregationalism is inadequate for the development of Christian strategy in the metropolis. Churchmen are beginning to perceive that in a society characterized by vast corporate structures and incredible social problems they must speak and act corporately.

The significance of this recognition for local councils of

churches clearly implies that in our metropolitan areas councils of churches must undergo substantial rethinking and restructuring. There is evidence that such changes are starting to take place. Given the existence of denominations, given the fact that denominations hold power in policy determination, given that there are financial and human resources which only the denominations can tap, the metropolitan council of churches which seeks to be a servant structure in our world must be constituted by the denominations themselves. The principle that local councils have to be composed of representatives of local churches is no longer viable in the metropolis.

Once it has been accepted that the council of churches in the city is a council of denominations, many problems can be ameliorated. For instance, the budgetary difficulties of local councils of churches grow out of the local church principle. Local churches have denominational goals for benevolence giving. These goals take priority over all outside giving. Thus, the typical local church will make a token gift to the council of which it is a part. Even this token gift will be conditional upon a council program which either pleases or is inoffensive to members of the church. This technique of financing contributes to programming within councils of churches aimed largely at providing pleasing services for supporting congregations.

Once it has been accepted that denominations are the constituent agents and are responsible for the financing of the council, ecumenical program and philosophy may undergo a substantial change. Now the council may recognize that services to local congregations are primarily the responsibility of the denominations; now the council itself may encounter the city from the posture of servanthood. Such a denominationally organized council of churches will not fear to speak and act on issues in the city. Nor will it hesitate to deal with corporate structures of power and status within the city.

Some will argue, at this point, that denominations are conservative institutions and that denominational executives are institutionalists whose primary concern is the maintenance of institutional strength. Such an argument does not adequately take into account the fact that, for all their moderation, denominations have been—almost without exception—more courageous in words and actions than the typical council of churches. Such arguments do not give evidence of a real understanding that the impotence of most local councils of churches is related to the fact that the denominational decision-makers are not a part of the decision-making processes within the metropolitan council.

This being said, however, it is clear that a council of churches structured on the basis of denominations must be committed to a range of freedom for program units within the council. The board of directors of a local council of churches structured on the denominational principle needs to be composed of denominational executives and denominational representatives charged with establishing broad policy, retaining staff, and providing budget. The program units of such a council must be made up of denominational representatives charged with pursuing vigorous ministry in the city, within the broad policies set by the council board.

A DENOMINATIONALLY ACCOUNTABLE COUNCIL

The Cleveland Council of Churches, organized within the last three years in a fashion similar to what we have been describing, has designated three commissions through which program is pursued. They are the Commissions on Public Witness, Ecumenical Education, and Metropolitan Affairs.

The Commission on Public Witness is concerned with the entire scope of the Gospel as disseminated through the mass media. Its director gives attention to the production of local radio and television programs, the placing of syndicated religious programs in these media, the maintenance of relationships with the religious news editors of the metropolitan dailies, the production of an ecumenical journal of news and opinion for the churchmen of the city, and ministry to professionals working in the mass media. The task of this commission is not the development of a public relations image for Protestantism, but the use of twentieth-century techniques for the communication of the Gospel of Jesus Christ.

The Commission on Ecumenical Education (in the writers' opinion poorly named) moves beyond what has normally been conceived as the Christian education function of councils of churches. Its director strives to bring together vocationally homogeneous groups—doctors, lawyers, businessmen, clerks, students—for reflection on their vocations from a Christian perspective. This commission, in addition, sets up opportunities for interdisciplinary small groups to meet around the concerns of professing Christians within the world of work. The commission utilizes the services of social scientists and people in the arts and humanities to assist in vocational-theological reflection.

The Commission on Metropolitan Affairs serves as a relevant social-action arm of organized Protestantism. The staff of this commission relates to the political leaders of the community, the civil rights leaders, police officials, and so forth. Each issue that comes before the city is scrutinized by churchmen competent in public affairs. In addition to the director of this department there are staff available in the areas of race and poverty, perhaps the two most significant issues on the current scene. The entire staff seeks to comprehend the hidden dynamics of the city and is committed to communicating data to clergy and laity alike.

In the structure identified above there is genuine potential for conflict. And yet, with a board composed of denominational decision-makers, and with commissions composed of denominational representatives, there is the possibility that the conflict may be positive, creative, and a genuine expression of the legitimate concerns of the Church. In controversy the council will be at least as strong as the weakest denomination; this is certainly stronger than the traditional council of churches has been.

The program units in the Cleveland Council have real freedom. A staff member is responsible first to the commission to which he is related, secondly to the board of the council through the council executive. The council executive sits as an ex officio member without vote on all the commissions. When he believes that the commission is pursuing a program contrary to the policies determined by the board of the council, he is responsible for bringing the commission and the board into dialogue with one another.

Of course, the board of such a council retains ultimate authority through its responsibility to allocate funds to the various program units. This authority extends to the salary levels of the staff of the commissions and to the program monies expended by the commissions. It also extends to the use of the council name. For example, the Commission on Metropolitan Affairs of the Cleveland Council, when supporting a rent strike in the ghetto, does so in the name of the Commission of the Churches on Metropolitan Affairs, and not in the name of the council itself. On issues where the council name is used by the program units, the board of the council must be consulted as to such usage and must concur.

There are several essential elements in a council of churches structured for servanthood in the world rather than service to the churches.

1. The denominations through their executives and appointed representatives must be responsible for the program and the financing of the council.

2. Program units must have freedom to act within certain boundaries, and to take positions with which all of organized Protestantism may not agree.

3. Staff members must relate primarily to the denominational representatives who sit on their commissions. Because each denominational representative sits on only one commission, he has the time necessary to develop sufficient background to act responsibly.

4. Denominational representatives on administrative boards, departments, and commissions must report regularly to, seek advice from, and involve the judicatory of the denomination

they represent. The council must be in every sense an instrument of the denominations for mission, rather than an instrument apart.

A council of churches seriously structured for mission will encounter the argument that it can never work. Certainly the history of co-operative Christianity in America has stressed the noncontroversial and the "least common denominator." Evidence is mounting that churches and denominations are now willing to have the co-operative arm of the Church engage in the struggles for justice in our world. For instance, when it became evident in 1963 that the civil rights revolution was pressing the issue of social justice upon the people of America, the National Council of Churches established a Commission on Religion and Race with a broad mandate for action. The unmistakable implication was that churches and churchmen through their ecumenical arm could and would involve themselves in the revolution. In this venture, denominational executives took the responsibility, leaders transcended their institutional concerns, and benevolence money was used for the purposes of civil rights.

In the metropolis there is no Methodist version of racial justice; no Baptist answer to unemployment; no exclusively Episcopal position as to what God is up to in the city. No single denomination, however effectively it can organize and administer local congregations, has either power or mandate to speak and act with authority for the Protestant community. Only a council of churches organized as an extension of the denominations for mission can really mount God's mission in the all-pervasive metropolis. The capacity to create such an instrument has been demonstrated; the mandate to do so throughout the metropolitan areas of our nation is before the Church.

CHAPTER 9

The More We Get Together

ABOUT 1910, and continuing into the 1920's—the years during which councils of churches were developing—a new movement appeared among the churches of rural and small-town America: the Larger Parish movement. The Larger Parish idea was, simply enough, the establishment of a co-operative relationship among a number of small congregations and the employment of a multiple staff to deal with the needs of the people and the several congregations. In this manner a small, struggling congregation, sharing the services of a number of trained men or women, could serve its community and parishioners more adequately. In discussing his experience in one of the early Larger Parishes, one minister commented, "We were two men and one woman, and we served five churches. We tried to achieve a degree of specialization in our ministry—one was good in music, another had a gift for work with Christian Endeavor. I devoted myself to calling. All of us preached."[2]

In the late forties and early fifties the group ministry migrated to urban America. In 1948, sensing the utter failure of the few remaining main-line Protestants in East Harlem to minister to the thousands of people in that community, a small group of students from Union Theological Seminary persuaded the exec-

[2] A comment made in conversation by the Rev. A. E. Wilson, of the Beneficent Congregational Church (United Church of Christ), Providence, R. I.

utives of four denominations to support a new mission. These four denominations, the American Baptists, Congregational Christians, Methodists, and Presbyterians, were joined shortly by the Reformed Church in America, the General Conference Mennonites, the Evangelical and Reformed Church, and the Evangelical United Brethren.

With funds thus provided on a broad interdenominational basis, a ministry to the very heart of the American city was born that has made a profound impact on the thinking of Protestantism about the city. Subsequent Parishes more or less based on the East Harlem model have grown up in Chicago, Cleveland, Oakland, New Haven, Boston, and several other cities.

The East Harlem project was launched in several storefronts. This choice of locale grew out of observations made by the staff of the East Harlem Protestant Parish: that (1) the store seemed to be a center of community life in East Harlem; (2) the plate-glass windows and street-level door made the storefront accessible and the activities that went on there readily observable by the people of the community; (3) numbers of such locations were available at modest rent, freeing funds for program and avoiding the typical inner-city facility problem of too much plant coupled with high maintenance and operating costs.

From its inception the ministry of the Harlem Parish assumed a variety of forms: the establishment of worshiping congregations where the Word was preached and the sacraments celebrated; the initiation of a pastoral ministry to the people of the community; the involvement of the staff of the Parish in serving the physical needs of community residents; the development of an action-oriented program involving both staff and people in the struggle against injustice.

The nurture of the worshiping congregation has been a major concern in the East Harlem Parish. In the early days, forms of worship were frankly experimental and on occasion bizarre. As the Parish has developed and matured there has been a growing emphasis on the more traditional forms of the Reformation. According to George W. Webber, one of the founders of the project, the proclamation of the Word is central in the service; Scripture and sermon are placed together; the minister preaches with the Bible open; reading and preaching are related to a study program participated in by small groups in the congregation.[3]

Holy Communion is an important element of the worship experience in East Harlem. The entire congregation seats itself around the Communion table, taking the bread and wine together. Although the sacrament is not celebrated every Sunday, the service of worship is considered abbreviated without its celebration. The service of offering which follows the sermon is the real beginning of the service of Holy Communion. Following the actual collection of money from the congregation, bread, wine, and money are brought forward and placed together upon the offering table, an act reminiscent of offertory liturgies in the primitive Church.

Baptism is part of the act of public worship and is seldom performed privately. The same may be said of marriage, which is performed along with the singing of hymns, the reading of Scripture, and the preaching of a sermon.

The pastoral role of the clergy of the East Harlem Protestant Parish does not differ substantially from the pastoral role in any congregation. The ministers call in the community, counsel their parishioners and the people of the community, teach, participate with them and instruct in small groups, and share with the individual families in the crises and joys of life. In the early days, the ministers met with open hostility and disinterest as they called in the apartments of East Harlem. The minister was identified as just another exploiter. Some of this opinion still exists, but the living testimony of a staff who actually live in the community and have demonstrated a genuine concern for people across the years has made for a remarkable measure of acceptance.

Concern for the people of East Harlem has taken this ministry

[3] George W. Webber, *God's Colony in Man's World* (Nashville: Abingdon Press, 1960), p. 61.

into areas which previously have been of peripheral significance to the Church, there or elsewhere. Over the years the Parish has sponsored a legal assistance program, a medical aid program, a credit union, a narcotics program, a camp for children in the countryside, and the distribution of food and clothing. Attorney William Stringfellow was, for a time, associated with this group ministry. In his book, *My People Is the Enemy*, he describes some of his work and frustrations in East Harlem. Stringfellow questions some of the early activities of the Parish. He says, "They plunged into all sorts of social work and social action—narcotics, politics, neighborhood improvement, education, housing, and the rest. . . . It was, in many ways, an admirable, if idealistic, and, in Christian terms, naïve effort. But they neglected and postponed the proclamation and celebration of the Gospel in East Harlem."[4]

While many of the efforts Stringfellow enumerates have continued in the Parish, it is the writers' observation that these are now (if not in the past) grounded in a view of the world and of man which is in keeping with the Gospel. Certainly the Word is proclaimed, the sacraments celebrated. Certainly the arrogant assumption that East Harlem Protestant Parish was *the* Church has given way to a modesty which allows for the possibility that God may be at work in other structures and places.

As in the early days, staff members in East Harlem continue to relate themselves with vigor to the civil rights movement, to neighborhood associations, to work on education, and to various political action groups. These efforts are seen by the ministry as their response to God's activity among men and may no longer be dismissed as the efforts of a group of naïve do-gooders to change the world.

We have already indicated that similar Parishes have developed in a number of other American cities. These "spin-offs" from East Harlem seem to have much in common with that ministry, but there is one substantial difference. The work of the East

[4] William Stringfellow, *My People is the Enemy* (New York: Holt, Rinehart and Winston, 1964), p. 88.

Harlem Protestant Parish is located in a neighborhood which includes an area of only a few square blocks; while as a community it embraces vast differences, it is geographically compact. In other cities, the Parish area may cover a major part of the metropolis. The work of group ministries in these cities tends to have a metropolitan scope, dealing with problems and concerns of the whole city and not simply with those of a compact and in some sense isolated neighborhood.

In spite of differences from community to community, it is possible to enumerate some of the characteristic qualities of the Parish movement in Harlem and elsewhere:

1. *The members of the group support one another* in a ministry of mutual involvement. They discuss their common problems, both vocational and personal. Sometimes they indulge in searing criticism of each other's traits. Wives of the ministers are included as full members of the group ministry, and the participation is as real as it is apparent. They may chair committees established by the group and often devote major time to Church and community projects as representatives of the group ministry. Members of the group socialize with one another and even seem to exclude "outsiders" from their social life. Frequent and regular meetings include specific periods of Bible study and prayer, discussion of the needs of particular churches, and attention to the problems of community and city. In short, the group becomes intensely supportive to its individual members, a fellowship of close friends who share concerns and frustrations, and are strengthened by the process.

Recently, the writers have had the opportunity of observing two who have left a group ministry to assume new responsibilities. One of these has had painful withdrawal symptoms. He misses the support of the group. His wife feels left out of his work. He seems to be compensating by intense attention to detail, a trait which his group frequently criticized him for *not* having. The other gives no evidences of a change in outlook or effectiveness. He likes the members of his group, but explains casually, "Every minister becomes part of a group of some sort which supports him, helps him, and chastens him when he needs it." He went on to comment of the friend who had experienced such agony on leaving the group, "He always attributed a special mystique to the group. But for me, it was never there."

2. *The members of the group share an economic discipline.* This means that staff members are supported at a level which allows all of them to live on approximately equal terms. The actual working out of the discipline is more complex than such a simple statement suggests. Many of the expenses that would come out of pocket for the minister of a typical denominational church are taken care of by administrative offices of the Parish. The Parish minister may never see his bills for rent, gas, electricity, and telephone service. Typically, the economic discipline calls for the staff member to forego the luxury of a family automobile. He is furnished a small bus or station wagon by the Parish. Even such incidentals as baby-sitting fees (the wife is member of the ministry, remember) and tuition for his children to attend private schools if public schools are inadequate may be part of the package.

The actual cash salary received by a Parish minister will be small, a base sum for the man, a little more if he is married, an allowance for each child based on age. In reality the level of total remuneration for each minister-family of a group ministry tends to exceed that received by the minister of a modest-sized church in a major denomination.

3. *The members of the group serve in areas of profound need:* neighborhoods of high unemployment, excessive crime rate, and pervasive poverty, where main-line Protestant churches are neither plentiful nor effective. By and large, today, Parishes localize their ministries in Church buildings which once housed middle-class congregations. As the neighborhood changed and the struggle to maintain a viable ministry became difficult, these churches were affiliated at the request of diocese or association with a developing Parish. Some storefronts remain in the Parish movement, but the trend is clearly to make use of conventional buildings.

In many neighborhoods where Parish churches are found, churches unrelated to the Parish continue to exist. It would be difficult today to distinguish the Parish church from the more relevant non-Parish congregation in the same neighborhood. This generalization, however, is probably accurate: Parish churches will tend to have a higher percentage of neighborhood people active in the congregations. Participants in the Parish mystique which has grown up in the last two decades would probably claim a great deal more for those congregations. As previously stated, there is no one inner city and no one inner-city church. The locale of the Parish church together with its constituency gives its program much of its character. Ministries in these neighborhoods will focus on emergency relief, open-air camping experience for children, and involvement with the welfare workers or police officials to a degree that would not be true in a denominational church in a more middle-class setting. Parish churches differ among themselves in program and emphasis.

4. *The members of the group live where they serve.* There is a strong feeling in virtually all the Parishes that the identification of the minister with the people of the community is essential if he is to serve effectively. Therefore he and his family will rent an apartment or a home in the very heart of the community. The minister is seen in the grocery store, the drugstore, the barbershop. He becomes known, as he moves through the community, as a neighbor. He stands alongside the people in a real and physical sense. He and his wife will be seen at the PTA, or at parents' night at the local school; he will be a participant in the neighborhood association or the political club; he may be found in the neighborhood bar.

In one dimension this presence is illusory, and the minister in the Parish movement is often criticized for it. He and his family are there by choice, not because they must be. He will leave that community as he moves on to other churches or ministries; he is *able* to move. His income is normally higher than that of his parishioners, his tastes probably more refined. His home is apt to be better furnished and his clothes newer and cleaner. In addition, as has already been pointed out, the Parish minister may actually send his children to a private school if he feels that education in the public school is inadequate. All these factors make, inevitably, for some distinction between the Parish minister and his constituency. Nonetheless, his presence in the community is real; his choice to spend most of his hours among the people he serves is obvious. That this has been a factor in the acceptance of Parish ministers in the communities where they serve is clear indeed.

5. *The members of the group receive ecumenical support.* Money, personnel, and other resources have poured into the Parish movement from most of the major denominational families in America. Although the ministers in the group and the congregations they serve usually carry denominational labels, support for the program is interdenominational: the National Board of Home Missions (by whatever name it may exist) of a denomination may send money to the Parish; the local judicatory of a denomination may aid the Parish in much the same way as it extends aid to its own needy congregations; Parish administration officials may be allowed or encouraged to solicit funds from affluent denominational congregations and their individual members.

At the present time substantial changes are taking place in the various Parish structures. Among these are some having to do with the shared economic discipline. Salaries based on tenure, merit, and need are the new order. As one ex-member who was in a group ministry from the days of its inception explains, "We were people passionately committed to ministry in the heart of the city. Most of us were just out of seminary. We had no highly structured organization which supervised us. Whatever we managed to collect from churches and individuals and denominations the group divided up—and if it went for salary it couldn't go for program." Now it is different! Boards of businessmen from the suburbs, ministers of suburban churches, and some representatives of the group ministry make the basic decisions which have to do with the life and ministry of the Parish. The unstructured, daring, sacrificial days seem a long distance behind us.

The Parish approach to ministry in the heart of the city has a clear appeal for many denominational officials and laymen, and Parish proponents have been especially skillful in promoting the more dynamic aspects of the ministry, especially the ecumenical overtones and opportunity for suburban lay support of ministry to the less fortunate. The appeal may well be related to a vague sense of guilt for having done so little to relieve suffering and to proclaim the Gospel close to home. Whatever the reason, denominations and local congregations have been singularly openhanded in giving support to the Parish movement, and there are many suburban laymen who are caught up in the Parish program rather than in the direct inner-city involvements of their own denominations.

The sobering fact is that until the birth of the East Harlem Protestant Parish the major denominations were guilty of ignoring the city at their doorstep. Some neighborhood houses in the slums had been operated, a few deep inner-city churches had received aid. For the most part the denominations had given little thought to ministry in the city or to the development of a strategy for such a ministry. Most denominations mindful of their own sin were glad to help the Parish movement get started —in some cases seizing upon it as an alternative to their own involvement. They were pleased to be able to turn over tired old buildings and struggling congregations to a Parish program. At one time, some Parish officials actually dreamed of operating all the churches of the major denominations in the inner-city core of a certain American metropolis.

DENOMINATIONS CATCH THE VISION

That particular dream has proved illusory. The Parish movement has proved to be a good teacher, and denominations have caught the vision of ministry in the city. Increasingly, they are making money and staff directly available to their churches. As previously observed, they have begun to hire "urban specialists" and to develop strategies for the city. These developments have caused tension between the denominations and the Parish.

The tensions are a direct outgrowth of the fifth characteristic of the Parish movement: its ecumenical support. Each of the Parishes, usually consisting of several local congregations, is directed by a group of laymen, ministers, and staff who are outside the established committee structure of the denominations. Key business leaders, leading professional men, and clergy of some well-known and influential churches make up the boards of the Parishes in the various cities across the country. The challenge to contribute to the betterment of their cities is one which these men have heard from many sources; in relating to the Parish movement they have been able to respond to that challenge within the context of the Christian faith.

Concern about the Parish movement revolves around this form of organization. The Parish boards are largely outside the denominational decision-making process. Despite the fact that denominational sources have contributed large sums to the movement, they are for the most part unrepresented *as denominations* on the boards of the Parishes. In the early days of the movement they were pleased simply to support the Parish programs, telling themselves that by so doing they were involved in the city. Now, however, that the denominations are showing concern for the city, some of them feel it imperative that they participate in the Parish decision-making process. This tension seems bound to grow in the years immediately ahead, as the major denominations take with increasing seriousness the challenge to relate to the metropolis. They may not view as responsible any use of denominational funds which is unrelated to, and not integrated with, the total urban ministry of the denomination.

However, some participants in the Parish movement look upon this separation from the denominational decision-making process as the most important factor in their ability to set up a mission to the city. Such Parish-oriented individuals insist that their type of structure makes for more radical freedom and mobility in programming—an argument which seems specious to these writers, given the business and social positions occupied by these key lay leaders in the Parish movement.

ANOTHER APPROACH TO GROUP MINISTRY

In recent years, a new approach to group ministries has begun to take place in a number of cities. Somewhat related to the Parish movement, and growing out of it, such ministeries are now to be found in a large number of cities: Atlanta, Denver, St. Louis, and so on. Unlike the Parish movement, these group ministries tend to be loosely structured. They may develop within a single denominational family or among neighboring congregations of several denominations. They are difficult to generalize about because of their wide variety of forms.

One outstanding example of these less-structured groups is the West St. Louis Ecumenical Parish. It comprises eleven churches of five denominations. Commencing in 1960, a group of clergy and laity in West St. Louis began to explore ways in which the Church might serve their broad neighborhood more effectively. They sought ways to unify the several and scattered witnesses of the Church, to learn from the skills and mistakes of others in their area as they sought to proclaim the Gospel, and to overcome the loneliness and frustration growing out of their efforts to relate to a large segment of a major metropolis.

The study brought forth a constitution providing for such co-operation. In 1961 the first meeting of the Parish Assembly was held—a group consisting of four delegates from each member church, and charged with jurisdiction over policies, programs, and activities of the West St. Louis Ecumenical Parish.

In the intervening period the work of this group has focused on Christian education (a lay school of theology, day camping, vacation Church schools), worship and fellowship (religious drama, pastor's Bible study, pastors' wives' study and fellowship), evangelism (religious census), community services (adult literacy training, youth employment services, tutoring services), casework, and action (local bond issue, school integration, housing).

These areas of co-operation and ministry reflect far more the typical Protestant Church ethos than that of the East Harlem Protestant Parish. This is probably related to the fact that the area served by the West St. Louis Ecumenical Parish is characterized by more stability, a higher economic level, and less social disorganization than a community like East Harlem. In addition, the co-operating churches retain substantial institutional strength. In the eleven co-operating churches there were over 8,500 members in 1965. The people served by these churches have interests and attitudes which call forth the type of program pursued in West St. Louis. An interesting evidence of the effect of this rather substantial remaining strength is the section of the constitution of the West St. Louis Ecumenical Parish which spells out: "Each participating body retains its own identity and autonomy in internal affairs. . . . It is understood that a church's decision not to take part in a particular project does not impair its membership in the Parish."[5]

Despite this loose and almost casual approach to co-operative ministry, the West St. Louis Ecumenical Parish has had an impact on its community. One observer summarized it in these terms: "They have accomplished the goal of turning the tide from blight and decay to conservation and renewal . . . they have joined with the West End Community Conference in battling through a citizen participation program to change urban renewal plans for the area . . . new schools have been built; the voice of the Negro in politics has been clearly heard, and many things have been happening because the people of the area have felt that the major denominations were with them."[6]

These ventures in group ministry point to the difficulty encountered by a single church or by a lone denomination in ministering to metropolis with its many faces. Few of the future expressions of group ministry are likely to take the form of the East Harlem Protestant Parish; more will undoubtedly have much in common with the West St. Louis Ecumenical Parish. The prin-

[5] From the constitution of West St. Louis Ecumenical Parish, Art. III, Sec. 2.
[6] From a letter to the authors by the Rev. Ray Bowden, Director of Church Social Work, St. Louis Presbytery.

cipal lessons of East Harlem, however, have been among the most important influences on the American Church in the last hundred years. From their example has come the commitment of most of the major denominations to minister in the city. The years ahead will undoubtedly see more sharing of ministry among local congregations; more acceptance of common disciplines in worship, study, and witness; and more discussion of the problems and strategy of urban ministry among clergy and laity, within and across denominational lines.

CHAPTER 10

Ministry to Captive Communities

THE traditional role of the chaplain has been that of pastor, friend, and counselor to "captive" communities—to those who through sickness, court sentences, or the obligations of military service are removed from home and immediate access to a church. In the absence of the home minister the chaplain stands in to serve. His work is an extension of the parish which has been left behind. When patient, prisoner, or soldier returns to the place of his choice from the place of his "captivity," the services of the chaplain are usually finished; he establishes no abiding congregation, but ministers to those who pass through the institution in which he serves. Although the college community is not a captive community in the same sense as a prison (some students might dispute this statement), the specialized institutional setting and brief term of residence of the student population place the campus ministry in a similar category.

The style of chaplaincy work in its institutional setting has been pastoral, one-to-one, and similar to the dialogue ministries in the sense of being deeply interpersonal. Historically, the chaplain has been a minister to individuals, and to individuals in their time of weakness, need, uprootedness, or all of these. When most people think of the chaplain they conceive of him almost exclusively in his pastoral role: visiting prisoners and patients, conducting bedside worship services, working with relatives of those who are institutionalized, serving as a liaison between the clergyman outside and the member of his congregation inside the institutional setting. Less known to the general public but equally significant is the supervision and training given by many chaplains to community clergy and seminary students. The typical institutional chaplain also serves as an interpreter of the institution to the community, and the other way around. In this community relations program he holds special seminars and orientation sessions.

There is no doubt that the role of the chaplain as thus described is an important and useful one. But as the director of the chaplains for the Diocese of Ohio, the Rev. Peter Goodfellow, explained to the writers, "There are not enough chaplains for all the hospitals and prisons. Many such institutions cannot afford a chaplain, and cannot be helped by churches who also cannot afford the outright gift of salary to the hospital. Many hospitals with the help of ministerial associations provide a rotating base of coverage through community clergy, but such a system provides coverage rather than full service. There is a manpower shortage, a lack of funds for support and training, and a shortage of trained chaplains."

The shortage of trained and ordained ministers for the chaplaincy is not really surprising. In our urbanized society, specialization is a fact in the institutional sector or system as in every other phase of residence and work. Institutions multiply, and their variety is staggering: juvenile diagnostic centers, schools for predelinquents, minimum- and maximum-security prisons, hospitals for the mentally ill, hospitals for general sickness, hospitals for communicable diseases, hospitals for chronic illness, hospitals for the crippled, metropolitan universities, business colleges, graduate professional schools, and graduate nursing schools —such a list only scratches the surface. As the number and size of these institutions continue to increase, the requests for trained chaplains capable of supervisory functions multiply. All of which suggests that the chaplaincy as generally conceived may not be a viable form of ministry in the near future. It will continue to exist, but in an isolated rather than a comprehensive sense.

Prediction based on present trends! The chaplain of the future will be increasingly involved in a ministry to those who man the structures of captive communities. In the area of health and welfare, even now the Church cannot carry out a ministry to individuals with special needs through its ordained clergy, whether these happen to be related to congregations or to service institutions. But Church laymen now man the staffs of private and public institutions at all levels, and are in daily contact with individuals who seek help from these agencies. If the Church has a ministry in the areas of health, welfare, and—of course—education, should it not be related to what its members are already doing in their vocational structures? This approach will use the ordained clergy of the Church for ministering to those who serve, rather than for directly serving patients, inmates, clients, or students to the exclusion of staff.

A broader vision of a ministry to the total university world is certainly emerging in university circles. Several campus Christian ministers known to the writers are reassessing the significance of their work with faculty and administrators, and are showing what must be described as new awareness of the total setting in which they work. One campus minister writes in his annual report, "I have made a point of establishing informal contact with both students and faculty, particularly at lunch time. This has awakened me to the need to become more a part of the day-to-day life of the university, and to become personally aware of the world view, personal concerns, and motivations of academic people, both students and faculty."[7]

WORLDS WITHIN THE WORLD

One way of looking at a chaplaincy is to see it as a ministry to a total institutional *gestalt*—a city within a city, a specialized microcosm which almost succeeds in creating and supporting a total life environment (not completely, since doctors go home at night, supplies are shipped in, and so forth). In this enclosed

[7] Quoted from "Student Christian Union of Cleveland, Fifteenth Annual Report," prepared by Gregory B. Taylor, member of staff.

context the chaplain ministers to a sometimes large but always limited group of people in interdependence and interaction. A chaplain who has this image of his ministry is already serving those who are self-sufficient (e.g. the staff) as well as those who are in need (e.g. the patients); he is relating to groups as well as to individuals. And as the number and complexity of institutions continues to outrun the supply of chaplains, he will increasingly minister through his relationships to the many echelons of personnel.

A ministry to the structures of health, welfare, and education fans out beyond the individual hospital, penal institution, or school. The hospital, for example, is part of an institutional system of hospitals. These institutions in turn are part of the health and welfare community, which is usually institutionalized in a community chest agency or welfare federation. The welfare organization receives support, leadership, ideas, and a sometimes heavy hand of reaction from the business and industrial complex. The hospital is also linked with governmental resources and controls at the metropolitan, state, and federal level. Start with a prison or a university, and a similar supportive and relational network is soon apparent. Considering the shortage of manpower and resources for chaplaincy work, the Church in metropolis may have to think more in terms of chaplaincies to the broader systems of which individual institutions are a part, and less in terms of chaplaincies to single institutions. The social welfare department of the typical metropolitan Church council, insofar as it emphasizes linkage and training rather than the operation of direct service programs, is in one particular way recognizing and realizing this ministry to the broader health and welfare sector of society.

There are more questions than answers as the chaplaincy seeks to function effectively in a burgeoning urban society. What does it mean to minister to institutional staff in their strength, equipping them in turn to minister through their vocations to their patients, inmates, clients, or students? How can these laymen, once trained and equipped, carry on a ministry that is

overtly Christian when they usually work in secular and governmental agencies? Should chaplains be denominational or attached
to a council of churches? Should they be parish-based or insti-
tution-based? Should they simply affirm the structures within
which they minister, or see themselves as agents of change and
reform?

FRONTIERS OF UNMET NEED

Determining its own role in metropolitan chaplaincy work is
only one of many problems confronting the Church in the total
field of health, education, and welfare. Detailed analyses of this
subject are going on within denominations and among the professionals working in the field; the authors will content themselves with such general observations as seem most relevant to
the subject of a total ministry of renewal in metropolis.

A basic observation which may help to delineate the ministry
of the Church in a positive as well as a negative way is this:
social welfare is not the same as action for social change; justice
and charity are not identical, and can be quite contradictory.

The Church of the Middle Ages became the most sinful
when in good intention it divorced charity for individuals in
need from social justice. This heresy of action is obvious when
the subject is the feudal lord and the object the land-locked
serf. It is not so obvious or unacceptable when the subject is the
suburbanite and the object the ghetto dweller (see earlier comments in Chapter 4, "Organizing for Change"). When the
Church in the contemporary metropolis divorces its concern
for private trouble from an equal concern for public issues, it
implies that the real business of the people of God is merely
charity and not social justice. The medieval heresy lingers on.

It must be remembered that many of the people who support
private and even public welfare in the city—who serve on the
boards of community chest councils, hospitals, and neighborhood
houses, to name just a few agencies—are quick death on any
social change which upsets the "power order" to which they

give their allegiance. As the executive director of a major division of a local welfare federation confessed off the record to one of the writers, "Don't hope to save the city through agencies like mine. Remember that welfare programs grew out of the custom of giving fruit and vegetable baskets at Christmastime. The same kinds of people are still involved."

A second observation is the following: society has undergone revolutionary changes which have left the Church with a marginal involvement in the direct sponsorship of health, education, and welfare agencies and programs. For a thousand years the Church was the primary welfare agency, but this is simply no longer true. The Church can react by bemoaning the number of institutions it has mothered which have somehow got away from the nest. It can complain that its distinctive witness has been snatched from it by increasing costs, accelerating specialization, galloping secularization, and massive governmental involvement. Or it can rejoice at the fact that society in general is assuming some of the Church's traditional responsibilities, and that the Church is now free to perform an unencumbered prophetic function in the metropolis.

The response of the Church to the pressing problems of general society must not be primarily institutional. Rather,

1. The corporate Church must promote justice in and through the general community. Our future will be determined by the kinds of decisions which are made for or against humanity in the complex structures of modern urban life. What counts is consistent and intelligent participation in, and pressure on, the structures of power where decisions are daily made. This means supporting those federal, state, and city programs which deal with the causes and not the symptoms of human misery: medical care for the aged, adequate unemployment compensation, adequate education, social security, job retraining, community organization, and community action programs which seek to change the structures of discrimination and poverty.

2. As long as the poor, needy, and sick are with us, the corporate Church must support those state- and community-

sponsored agencies which deal directly with human suffering. Although social welfare is not the same as social action, it will be needed until social action is successful. And even in that far-off and blessed day, mental and physical sickness will still be with us. Modern welfare and health programs call for professional skills which the Church, as such, does not possess, and resources of which the Church has only a fraction. Piety, good will, and a proper theological perspective are not substitutes for professional competence in operating health and welfare agencies.

3. For purposes of research to determine proper action—for purposes of informing the Church community concerning the extent of specific social problems—and for purposes of dramatizing a need and its viable solution or amelioration—the Church has a limited role in direct health, welfare, and educational services. When the Church sponsors an institutional program for the avowed purpose of raising standards and demonstrating excellence, it must be certain that the excellence can be recognized by others than the promoters of the program. Staff must be employed on the basis of their qualifications rather than because they are ministers. Most important: when any program of a health, welfare, or educational nature becomes a substitute for action rather than a spur, it should be discontinued.

In the absence, or in anticipation, of needed public or community-supported services, the Church has a pioneering role in establishing such services as temporary parts of its program. When the broader community is willing to adopt these agencies and services, they should be phased out or turned over to community sponsors.

Translated into the concrete and specific, this limited-approach philosophy suggests that an urban judicatory or Church council may operate or relate to a neighborhood house in a deprived neighborhood, to a home for the aged, a general hospital, a casework referral agency, a family counseling bureau, or some other service agency. But the agency should carry on a quality program with top-flight staff. It should serve as a window through which the Church can look upon a section of the spectrum of human suffering and deprivation and learn from the confrontation. The agency should not be duplicated endlessly across city and state, as is being done with homes for the affluent-aged. And above all, the agency should be one which, instead of simply duplicating services available down the street, is ministering on a frontier of unmet need.

PART V

Organizing for Renewal: Conclusion

The Organizational Bias

TOO many of the books that analyze and describe the ministry of the Church of Jesus Christ in metropolis write *finis* before arriving at the subject matter of this Conclusion. The gravely ill patient—namely, the Church in its urban setting—is laid out upon the operating table. The incision is made and the troubled region exposed. A careful and detailed analysis is carried out of the nature and extent of the illness. Then the incision is sewed up, antiseptic generously sprinkled on the stitches, and the diagnostician-surgeon, either lamenting the near-terminal state of the patient or rejoicing that the illness proved to be only skin deep, goes about his business.

If a therapy is projected for the patient, it is usually in terms of "Do this or that, and you shall live." Seldom is any real attention given to a step-by-step description of treatment; who might be responsible for administering it; how much the projected care will cost; the duration and extent of the prescribed therapy; and whether it will make a significant difference in the health of the patient. The wistful hope seems to be that someone, somewhere, will assume the continuing role of healer through the mere conviction that an accurate diagnosis has been made. This hope is tempered by the feeling (sometimes implied, often spelled out in detail) that those officially in charge of the health of the patient—the committees and staffs of the denominational families—are bureaucratic bumblers.

Although this may sound like a parody, it comes frighteningly close to the truth. The allusions in the allegory are obvious.[1] Many of the sociologically oriented theologians and theologically oriented sociologists, writing the books that diagnose the sickness of the Church in the metropolitan community, seem either largely unaware or completely skeptical of the Church as organization and Body. There is an unreality in their oversight, especially as these same writers often show positive appreciation for an urban society characterized by pragmatic specialization, for that amazing instrument for achieving limited and proximate goals called "organization," and for the vast and growing knowledge of techniques of motivation and management. The Church, after all, has its corporate structures which are just as essential to experimentation, implementation, and interpretation as those of any secular-based organization. The possibility of using these structures to revitalize the life of the Church and develop a ministry with relevance for the metropolis does not occur to—or is rejected by—these analysts.

The concern of this book is not rooted in denominational pride: "It's better to be a _____ than a _____" (the reader may fill in the blanks with his own denominational biases). Rather, it grows out of an attempt to understand the structures of the Church and to use those structures for mission.

---

[1] There are a few exceptions. Among the writers who deal in a positive fashion with the church as organization is Paul Moore, Jr., *The Church Reclaims the City* (New York: The Seabury Press, 1964). His comments on the role of diocese, district, and presbytery are especially helpful. Another exception is Walter Kloetzli, *The Church and the Urban Challenge* (Philadelphia: Muhlenberg Press, 1961). Colin Williams in *Where in the World* (paperback; New York: National Council of Churches, Office of Publication and Distribution, 1963), gives a lengthy footnote to the central role of the board and agency in mission, but does not elaborate further (p. 9).

Organizing the Judicatory

for Mission

UNLESS the administrative machinery of the Church is put to work rather than ignored or bypassed, widespread renewal will not be forthcoming. Insofar as relevance has been achieved on more than a chance or occasional basis, responsible Church administration has been involved. The Church in the metropolis, above all, needs competent staff, committed to renewal. It also needs wise policy, sound procedure, and an organization which puts people, programs, and money to work.

Along with the widespread concern for rediscovering the missionary structure of the congregation there needs to be at least as much concern for the missionary structure of the association, diocese, or presbytery that serves the metropolis. As the winds of change blow, chilling some expressions of Christian community and breathing new life into others, those who are concerned for Church renewal need to see that some winds blow in the direction of the Church judicatories. As a matter of fact this is already happening, as denominational units realize that they have responsibilities in mission beyond playing musical chairs with their ministers and churches and throwing buckets of spiritual sand on brush fires in local congregations.

The job to be done must be determined prior to development of the structure to do it. A clear vision should precede both. The self-image envisioned by the metropolitan denomination must be more expansive than it has been, with its traditional focus on "housekeeping" services to self-supporting local congregations. The denominational unit must see itself as a platform for developing and executing a total ministry to the metropolis, a ministry sensitive to the ever shifting challenge and crisis of the secular city. Developing a total ministry to the metropolis requires a structure for mission, a system for mission, and a staff for mission. All three deserve careful attention.

Structure for Metropolitan Mission

There is no single best way to organize the committee and program structure of a metropolitan judicatory. The polity of the particular denomination must be carefully considered. Denominations in the free church tradition may need a different format from those with an episcopal structure. The size of the metropolis served, the number of communicant members in the judicatory, the extent of financial resources, and the nature and scope of present program involvement are other significant factors. Beyond these "givens," the goal of the denomination must be to build into structure a flexibility which will allow for response in the name of Christ to the needs of the world. As the world and time write the agenda, the judicatory must be able to read, assimilate, and reply.

One possibility is the establishment of two major program committees (or commissions) corresponding to the two major targets of mission. The first of these committees would be concerned with aiding local congregations in their Christian education, evangelism, social action, and other concerns. Congregations with special needs and problems, such as the churches "farther in" mentioned earlier, would be related to this committee. The survey function, planning function, strategy function, and evaluation function, insofar as these relate to residential congregations, could be located at this point in the judicatory structure and assigned to subcommittees or special task forces.

A second committee (or commission) would be responsible for the judicatory mission itself, and would represent a genuine innovation for most metropolitan denominational units. Program concerns would cut across the traditional divisions of Christian education, evangelism, social witness and action, and home or national missions, in the process giving a much-needed unity to mission in the metropolis.

This second program committee would furnish representatives to the supervisory boards of church councils and to the specialized ministries to issues or structures—denominational or ecumenical—supported by the denomination. If the judicatory operates a Christian education center or camp, this would be as much a responsibility of the committee as a chaplaincy or a program in religion and race. The committee would take on the tasks of long-range planning and short-range strategy in relationship to nonresidential ministries.

Obviously some important judicatory duties, such as ministerial placement, would not be subsumed in this two-committee suggestion and would require additional structure. It would also be necessary to unify ministry through the local congregations with the metropolitan ministries carried on directly by the judicatory. This might require a co-ordinating council or committee.

Another possible structure for the judicatory in mission is one which simply creates task forces to deal with significant programs, projects, and issues confronting the judicatory. Such *ad hoc* task forces would be organized to fulfill a purpose and disbanded when the mission is accomplished. The plan would substitute for the usual broad-content committees, such as Christian education and social education and action, such separate task forces as religion and race, unemployment and poverty, dropouts and delinquency.

SYSTEM FOR MISSION

A structure has significance only when it is put to work. The best way to develop a structure for mission is to look at the various functions of the judicatory as it engages in actual program, and then see where these functions can be built into a working structure.

First, there is the sensitivity function—a function difficult to program. Active involvement in the life of the community and its organizations by clergy and laity of the metropolitan denomination, coupled with regular conferences devoted to reflection on the needs and problems of the metropolis, will build the sensitivity function into judicatory life. Pure research is probably not the ongoing function of the metropolitan judicatory—i.e., cutting deeply into a problematic slice of metropolitan life without any clearly-defined purpose for subsequent findings. It makes more sense to utilize through continuing survey and study the research documents prepared by city and county planning commissions, metropolitan welfare federations, and those ecumenical research and planning agencies which are increasingly a part of the urban church scene.

Second, there is the planning function. Most urban judicatories perform poorly in this area. There is no magic involved: the stuff of statistics, trends, needs, and possible answers are fed into a study-and-discussion process. As perspective clarifies, concerns are lifted up. A concern is simply an issue or problem which in the opinion of the planning group merits special attention. Concerns, through continuing study and probing, are translated into policies. A policy is a statement of intention: This is what the judicatory intends to do. Policies are guidelines for mission. If they are confirmed by the judicatory decision-makers, policies lead to programs which may involve staff and the expenditure of program money. The wise planning group develops priorities in concerns and programs. The effort to do everything usually leads to doing nothing.

A planning group should be small and should meet frequently. Qualifications include a broad knowledge of both denomination and city, and the ability to handle abstractions. Many planning processes bog down in the immediacies of strategy. The group should think months and even years ahead. When a program is decided upon, the planners should turn the details over to those responsible for a strategy of implementation.

Third in logical progression comes the strategy function, which might also be called the operational phase. Those who plan new programs probably should not be the same people who supervise ongoing program, although they may be members of a different subcommittee of the same parent committee. Strategy involves the development of an over-all approach to ministry in the metropolis, taking into account the work both of the individual denomination and of other denominations in the community. Strategy involves the supervision of those congregations, denominational projects, and ecumenical agencies which make up the total ministry of the denominational unit. Strategy involves the review and evaluation of ongoing program. On the basis of insight gained in actual day-by-day operation, suggestions go back into the judicatory structure responsible for the planning function. The movement is rotary; feedback leads to the development of new thrusts in mission.

Fourth, the evaluative function is significant enough to be singled out for mention, although it probably should be handled by those responsible for strategy. Evaluation, like planning, is as much art as science. Because subjectivity enters in, and individuals ride mission hobbyhorses, evaluation should never be made by one person. Whenever possible, guidelines related to the concerns and policies developed in the planning process should be utilized in making evaluations.

Fifth, the resource function is a crucial one. This divides neatly into a trustee phase and what might be called an interpretation and cultivation phase. There is a continuing question in most judicatories as to whether trustees should be the same people as those responsible for program. When they are involved in program responsibilities, trustees usually do not see themselves as men divinely ordained to guard the moneybags from program-intoxicated spendthrifts. On the other hand, people skillful in monetary affairs are not always the best qualified for the program phases of mission. It is possible to make a sharp demarcation between desirability (a strategy responsibility), and feasibility (a trustee function). When the trustees have no program involvement they are limited to determining whether the money is ready and available.

The promotion and interpretation of mission is often slighted by the metropolitan judicatory. Every Church member needs to know and has the right to know where his money is going and why he should give sacrificially. This requires a year-round educational program, with such interpretative material as film strips and brochures in constant production.

In many churches there are people who are critical of the use of missionary monies for administrative purposes. Often, these same people are loyal and even enthusiastic about the mission enterprise of the Church in Asia, Africa, or Latin America. There needs to be careful interpretation of the fact that money spent on administration in Hoboken, for example, is not "overhead" but is for the purpose of enabling the ministry of the Church to be more effective.

Sources for funding the mission differ from denomination to denomination. In addition to allocations from national and state sources, many judicatories now have their own "cause" programs. Local churches give to the judicatory treasury. Through a process of evaluation, priorities are developed and budgets allocated from the judicatory base. The "cause" program is often comparable to that of a community chest. For instance, in the case of a local congregation giving directly to a neighborhood house supported by the denomination, the gift would be subtracted from the total amount the neighborhood house can expect to receive from the judicatory. This puts the direction of program development where it belongs, in the hands of the judicatory. The agency with dramatic local appeal or a high-pressure promotional system does not receive a disproportionate share of the mission dollar.

There is one serious danger in local "cause" programs. The wealthy metropolitan unit of the denomination can usually support its own mission, but the unit in a less affluent region of the nation, which cannot underwrite the mission within its boundaries, suffers if money is not first forwarded to a national board for distribution. There are ways to handle this imbalance. On a percentage basis, fixed by the judicatory or suggested to the local congregations, some money may be spent locally and the rest sent directly to national headquarters for allocation in this nation and abroad.

STAFF FOR MISSION

The need for specialized staff in the metropolitan judicatory was mentioned early in these pages. It is important that key positions should not be awarded to those skillful in oiling the nuts and bolts of the ecclesiastical enterprise, nor to those who see their mandate as simply that of "holding the Church together"— which, interpreted, means avoiding all controversial encounters with the demands of the world for revolution and reform.

The United Presbyterian Church now employs eighteen metropolitan specialists across the nation. The United Church employs fifteen. Other denominations follow apace. In one Midwestern city in 1965, five denominations employed staff specialists responsible for specialized ministries and inner-city churches: the United Presbyterian, the United Church of Christ, the Methodist, the Evangelical United Brethren, and the American Baptist. These staff members were in addition to senior denominational executives such as bishops, district superintendents, and association ministers whose responsibilities are broader and more general.

Many denominations also employ Church and community staff, "issue" specialists, on a regional or metropolitan level; consultants in new church development; and field staff in Christian education. Administrative and adjunct staff, whatever their specific job descriptions, need a knowledge of the metropolis as the context and focus of mission. Christian education, for example, must be increasingly understood as a program discipline which involves far more than consultation with suburban Church-school leadership and the development of youth programs in local congregations. Education takes place in issue- and structure-oriented ministries, vocational groups, inner-city congregations, wherever the Church is in mission. If he is to be an effective consultant, the judicatory-based Christian educator needs information and skills beyond those traditionally to be found in his specialized discipline.

An example in point, of structuring, systematizing, and staffing for mission in metropolis, would seem to be in order. The urban executive of a metropolitan judicatory in an eastern city some years ago attended a regional denominational meeting. There he learned that the churches in one city were having real success in getting the political powers to recognize the importance of having the poor represented on the governing board of the then new "anti-poverty" program. His denomination, in his own city, had for some years been concerned about developing a valid ministry among the poor but had not known how to proceed.

When he returned home this urban executive discussed the matter with the urban missioners of several denominations. Together with leaders from the civil rights groups and the staff of an interdenominational mission agency, they began to press the mayor of the city to broaden the antipoverty board to include representation from the poorer neighborhoods.

At the same time the planning committees of several denominations, together with the interdenominational agency, began to consider the development of a new ministry to poverty. A plan was drawn up to hire a staff person to work full time to help citizens living in poverty to help themselves, and to relate to members of the more affluent churches around the problems of the poverty-stricken in that city. Ultimately it was determined that such a ministry had priority, and resources were found in four denominations and a foundation to establish such a program. A job description was written, spelling out the lines of responsibility. A special board was established made up of representatives of the several denominations and the interdenominational agency.

The policy of the new ministry, as enunciated by its board, was to organize and staff in such a way as to develop a relationship between the Church, the government program, and the poor. The work of the staff man is supervised by the board, and the denominational representatives on the board report to their various judicatories. The missions committees of the judicatories review the work of this specialized ministry, evaluate it in terms

ple in point, of structuring, systematizing, and staffing
n in metropolis, would seem to be in order. The urban
of a metropolitan judicatory in an eastern city some
attended a regional denominational meeting. There he
at the churches in one city were having real success in
political powers to recognize the importance of having
represented on the governing board of the then new
rty" program. His denomination, in his own city, had
years been concerned about developing a valid ministry
poor but had not known how to proceed.
he returned home this urban executive discussed the
h the urban missioners of several denominations. To-
h leaders from the civil rights groups and the staff of
nominational mission agency, they began to press the
the city to broaden the antipoverty board to include
ion from the poorer neighborhoods.
me time the planning committees of several denomina-
ther with the interdenominational agency, began to
development of a new ministry to poverty. A plan
up to hire a staff person to work full time to help
ng in poverty to help themselves, and to relate to
the more affluent churches around the problems of
-stricken in that city. Ultimately it was determined
ministry had priority, and resources were found in
inations and a foundation to establish such a program.
iption was written, spelling out the lines of respon-
pecial board was established made up of represent-
several denominations and the interdenominational

of the new ministry, as enunciated by its board,
ize and staff in such a way as to develop a relation-
the Church, the government program, and the
ork of the staff man is supervised by the board, and
ational representatives on the board report to their
atories. The missions committees of the judicatories
ork of this specialized ministry, evaluate it in terms

programs probably should not be the same people who supervise ongoing program, although they may be members of a different subcommittee of the same parent committee. Strategy involves the development of an over-all approach to ministry in the metropolis, taking into account the work both of the individual denomination and of other denominations in the community. Strategy involves the supervision of those congregations, denominational projects, and ecumenical agencies which make up the total ministry of the denominational unit. Strategy involves the review and evaluation of ongoing program. On the basis of insight gained in actual day-by-day operation, suggestions go back into the judicatory structure responsible for the planning function. The movement is rotary; feedback leads to the development of new thrusts in mission.

Fourth, the evaluative function is significant enough to be singled out for mention, although it probably should be handled by those responsible for strategy. Evaluation, like planning, is as much art as science. Because subjectivity enters in, and individuals ride mission hobbyhorses, evaluation should never be made by one person. Whenever possible, guidelines related to the concerns and policies developed in the planning process should be utilized in making evaluations.

Fifth, the resource function is a crucial one. This divides neatly into a trustee phase and what might be called an interpretation and cultivation phase. There is a continuing question in most judicatories as to whether trustees should be the same people as those responsible for program. When they are involved in program responsibilities, trustees usually do not see themselves as men divinely ordained to guard the moneybags from program-intoxicated spendthrifts. On the other hand, people skillful in monetary affairs are not always the best qualified for the program phases of mission. It is possible to make a sharp demarcation between desirability (a strategy responsibility), and feasibility (a trustee function). When the trustees have no program involvement they are limited to determining whether the money is ready and available.

The promotion and interpretation of mission is often slighted by the metropolitan judiciary. Every Church member needs to know and has the right to know where his money is going and why he should give sacrificially. This requires a year-round educational program, with such interpretative material as film strips and brochures in constant production.

In many churches there are people who are critical of the use of missionary monies for administrative purposes. Often, these same people are loyal and even enthusiastic about the mission enterprise of the Church in Asia, Africa, or Latin America. There needs to be careful interpretation of the fact that money spent on administration in Hoboken, for example, is not "overhead" but is for the purpose of enabling the ministry of the Church to be more effective.

Sources for funding the mission differ from denomination to denomination. In addition to allocations from national and state sources, many judicatories now have their own "cause" programs. Local churches give to the judicatory treasury. Through a process of evaluation, priorities are developed and budgets allocated from the judicatory base. The "cause" program is often comparable to that of a community chest. For instance, in the case of a local congregation giving directly to a neighborhood house supported by the denomination, the gift would be subtracted from the total amount the neighborhood house can expect to receive from the judicatory. This puts the direction of program development where it belongs, in the hands of the judiciary. The agency with dramatic local appeal or a high-pressure promotional system does not receive a disproportionate share of the mission dollar.

There is one serious danger in local "cause" programs. The wealthy metropolitan unit of the denomination can usually support its own mission, but the unit in a less affluent region of the nation, which cannot underwrite the mission within its boundaries, suffers if money is not first forwarded to a national board for distribution. There are ways to handle this imbalance. On a percentage basis, fixed by the judicatory or suggested to the local congregations, some money may be spent locally and the rest of the goals originally set by the board and in comparison with other projects and ministries in the city, and allocate funds for its work.

In this brief example we see all the considerations discussed in this section at work: structure, system, and staff for mission. It is clear that the mission of the Church of Jesus Christ in the metropolis will not just happen. That mission must be perceptively planned and supervised, or an individual breakthrough here and there will flare brightly, flame briefly, and flicker out.

Organizing in the Inner City

THE denominations should be grateful to such extradenominational ventures as the East Harlem Protestant Parish for dramatizing the Protestant withdrawal from the "difficult" neighborhoods of the city, and for demonstrating the possibility of keeping resident congregations alive and relevant. Now it is time for the denominations to assume responsibility for congregational ministries in the midtown and uptown of Metropolis, U.S.A. There is evidence that this responsibility is being assumed, and that it is more than a fad among the major denominations.

More can be done, and the frontier is now administrative as well as experimental. How does the metropolitan unit of a denomination so mobilize and utilize its resources that residential congregations in low-income neighborhoods receive a high priority for mission, and are enabled to minister effectively to their communities? Here are some step-by-step suggestions.

A Marriage for Mission

What is the process by which a denomination decides to stand behind certain of its churches in changing urban situations, initiate new ministries in others, and close out others? There are no hard-and-fast rules, but there are guidelines. The denomination must not act like Browning's Caliban, the capricious primitive who played God on a sandy beach, letting this crab pass unscathed, pulling a pincer off the next one, and crushing another under his horny heel.[2] Rather it should develop and apply broad policy which gives objectivity to the process.

Although the involvement of the denomination with a local inner-city church is usually triggered by financial trouble in the local congregation, it is far better to identify churches with special needs and problems by studying a broad section or quadrant of the city ecumenically or denominationally. If this requires specialized staff work and other expenses, the denomination must be willing to underwrite the bill. Many denominations provide self-study guides which help the church to analyze itself in its community setting. Such analysis is a useful tool in developing a perspective for denominational support. Whether the local church or the judicatory initiates the process, the local church should be expected to study its financing, programming, and staff; to define its service or parish area; to analyze the various components in its unique community setting; and to enumerate the number and variety of other churches within a specified area.

On the basis of this self-study and whatever other information is available, denominational representatives and local church leaders should define the unique mission of this particular congregation, considering at the same time other alternatives to strengthening the ministry of the church, such as merger or dissolution. A completed statement of unique mission should incorporate a pledge that this congregation is willing to serve, witness to, and welcome all people of the general parish area who are responsive to the ministry of the congregation. The statement should also indicate a willingness on the part of local church leadership to consult on a continuing basis with the proper agencies of the denomination concerning staff, program, and capital needs. The total congregation should be made aware of, and should be in accord with, the statement of unique mission.

At all times the denominational representatives should make

[2] Robert Browning, "Caliban upon Setebos; or, Natural Theology in the Island," *Complete Works* (New York: The Macmillan Company, 1941).

it plain that financial help is neither a favor nor a punishment, that if granted it does not reduce a church to second-class status, and that it is given to strengthen the relevant ministry of the total Church in situations where a local congregation has more vision than resources. Unless the church understands why it is receiving aid, and accepts the ground rules, the process is pointless and will only delay the death throes.

The following check list should prove helpful to denominational decision-makers seeking criteria for the support of particular inner-city churches or ministries:

1. *Vision.* Does local leadership have a reasonably concrete vision of ministry to the community? Do present members, even if most of them live at a distance, really have an interest in the people and problems of the church neighborhood?

2. *Performance.* Has the congregation demonstrated by past performance that their problem is one of inadequate resources rather than disinterest in any ministry which goes beyond institutional survival and self-service?

3. *Inclusiveness.* Does this congregation enthusiastically support an open-door policy of ministry and service? Has it indicated through past activities that it is willing to welcome everyone out of commitment rather than desperation?

4. *Community.* Are there enough people in the parish area served by the church (in relationship to other priorities) to justify a supported ministry? Are the incomes of neighborhood people, the size of the congregation, and the extent of the projected services such that aid rather than an intensive stewardship program is indicated?

5. *Duplication.* Would the ministry of this congregation be missed if it were closed or relocated—i.e., are there congregations of the same or similar denominations in the immediate neighborhood which are serving effectively, and which duplicate the work of this congregation? Should this congregation merge with a nearby congregation of the same denomination, and if merger is a live option, and this congregation is reluctant, does it deserve unilateral support?

6. *Prognosis*. Is this congregation at all likely to be effective in implementing the unique ministry it envisions? (Number, age, and attitude of members are significant factors.) Is the building in which the congregation meets suitable for its projected ministry? (State of repair, expense of upkeep, and rooms suitable for community activity are significant factors.)

7. *Ecumenicity*. Should this congregation develop a ministry in co-operation with neighboring churches of other denominations to merit aid? Should the congregation join in the ministries of the ecumenical agencies in the city?

8. *Staffing*. Does this particular situation justify a full-time pastorate? A multiple staff? (Obviously, only in rare instance should aid be given to part-time pastorates.) Is this pastorate one which an able minister will see as a challenge because of the scope and value of the work to be done? If presently staffed, is the minister one who will aid or impede a program expanded through aid? If the pulpit is vacant, or when it becomes vacant, will this congregation co-operate with the judicatory in securing community-oriented staff?

FINANCES AND THE AIDED CONGREGATION

In the dollar market of the sixties few inner-city churches can operate effectively with a current expense budget of less than $20,000, and $30,000 would be a fairer figure. It is impossible to provide adequate staff, maintain a building, and carry on a program for less. Sometimes urban churches struggle along on less money by ignoring building needs, but delayed maintenance only puts off the day of financial reckoning.

The high cost of operating a viable residential congregation in the inner city means that any one denomination is limited in the number of residential parishes it can aid. The only alternative is to dribble out money to every local congregation facing financial hard times. As suggested elsewhere, mission money expended casually on a weak church, the ministry of which is irrelevant or totally institutional, can only extend for a brief period the life of that church. The denomination must decide where it has a stake in witness. And this of course involves communication with other denominations to set up spheres of responsibility, in this case neighborhoods in the heart of the metropolis. Forms of co-operation among denominations in which areas of responsibility for mission are carefully delineated have more chance of success in the heart of the city than in the high-dollar-return suburbs.

Attention needs to be given to the question of whether the local church is an adequate unit for financing. Pressed to its ultimate conclusion, this position really says that main-line Christianity is for "clients" who can pay for it. Historically, denominations have approached the programming and staffing of their financially embarrassed churches as old Procrustes confronted his guests, chopping off hands and feet to make the body fit the bed.

Lyle Schaller, in *Planning for Protestantism in Urban America,* suggests that no single elementary school depends on the neighbors and parents in the immediate vicinity to pay the taxes which operate that particular school.[3] The base is broadened, the load is shared, and the school in the poor neighborhood benefits from the taxes paid in the wealthier sectors of the school district. Schaller wonders if denominations might not learn from the public schools. Denominations are obviously not ready to pool all the resources of their local churches and then allocate to each congregation on the basis of need. A step which they can take in this direction is the responsible allocation of money for those inner-city congregations where need exceeds ability to pay.

A troubling question is whether financial aid cripples the initiative of local members and makes them overly dependent on outside help. There is a problem here, but it is overstated and overrated. Co-operation in mission between denomination and local congregation, properly interpreted, can actually save a congregation from that parochial pride which leads to loyalty to a particular institution rather than to mission.

The authors know of one congregation which has developed

---

[3] Lyle Schaller, *Planning for Protestantism in Urban America* (Nashville: Abingdon Press, 1965), p. 163.

an interesting compromise between the goals of self-support and adequate ministry. The local budget is divided into two categories: "a community-center program" and "a Church" program. Local membership is challenged to support the Church program with the clear understanding that the full support of this block of the total program represents "self-support." The community-center program is interpreted as a service their denomination has requested them to engage in and direct as part of the total denominational mission in the city. Members do not expect to underwrite the community-center program financially (except as they give their share to the central benevolence program of the denomination). Through this interesting approach, self-support becomes a realizable goal. It represents what a local congregation would pay for a pastor, the minimum upkeep of a building, and a skeleton program. Through co-operation in the community center the local church sees itself as an agent of mission rather than an object of mission.

Staffing the Inner-City Congregation

One of the hopeful signs in developing mission through inner-city congregations is the number of young ministers who see the church "farther in" as a genuine frontier. Scarcely a week goes by that a letter does not cross the desk of one or the other of the writers from a minister who wants to serve a church in the basin of the city rather than in the suburbs. This may well represent a misunderstanding of metropolis, where increasingly suburb and city are bound together in common problems and mutual dependency. Nevertheless, there are more men interested than there are openings, and the situation is reminiscent of the enthusiastic response among young Christians in the early twentieth century to the challenge to world mission: "the world for Christ in our generation."

The question of salary level is a difficult one. One approach is to correlate the minimum salary of a minister in an aided church with the beginning salary paid to new church development ministers in the area served by the denominational unit. At least as much skill is needed to develop program in the inner city as in a new church in a high-priority suburb, and the new church minister can anticipate significant raises from his congregation within five years of organization. In a process of regular review between denominational representatives and local church leaders the salary of the minister should be discussed, and regular raises should be encouraged on the basis of merit and tenure.

The education of children has been more honestly confronted in the foreign mission than in the home mission field. Many men leave the inner city during the time their children are in school because they find neighborhood schools inadequate. A program of supplementary educational support to provide private education as needed for the children of inner-city pastors is a must as the denomination allocates its money. Policy on this needs to be set by denominational leaders. Although the issue is submerged, it will usually surface when a pastor who lives in a deprived neighborhood unburdens himself. The sacrifice of his children is not part of his commitment.

Suburban ministers often resent denominational support of a multiple staff in a small church of two hundred members when they serve six or seven hundred members by themselves and still meet denominationally set dollar goals for mission projects. Staff cannot be measured simply against membership. In addition to all the reasons for multiple staff underscored earlier, the number of full-time professional staff serving churches in the typical inner city is lower in proportion to the population than the number of full-time staff in the suburbs. If it is true that the suburban pastor has a heavy load of counseling, leadership education and recruiting, and general administration, his burden is not complicated by the special problems faced by people on low and even subsubsistence income.

If structure follows function, the inner-city church should hire staff and develop staff responsibilities on the basis of the particular mission of the congregation being served, and the unique services needed to implement the task. For instance, one church may want to utilize the talents of a combination Christian education and community center director with a two-year-beyond-A.B. degree called "Master in Church Social Work." Another church may employ a visiting health nurse; still another a public housing visitor, an athletic young man who might be called a neighborhood recreation director, or someone vaguely called a "parish worker." A grouping of denominational inner-city churches in Wilmington, Delaware, shares a caseworker who assists the ministers in their counseling load and makes referrals to the accredited social work agencies. An inner-city council of four churches in San Francisco, in addition to "lead" pastors, hires a social worker, a minister of Christian education, and an evangelist. A congregation in Greenwich Village has a minister on the staff who gives full time to the arts, and the congregation sponsors a theater, ballet groups, and frequent exhibitions. Many churches which operate intensive Saturday programs for neighborhood children hire numerous schoolteachers on a weekend basis. The theory is that a multiple staff is really only needed when the church program peaks.

One of the trends worth mentioning, which is sure to expand in the next few years, is the use of laymen with certain kinds of professional competence in the city church. Increasingly, churches are recognizing that many unordained men and women have both the commitment and the training to provide creative leadership for specialized ministries within the Church. The idea that only the ordained are capable of working in the Church or Church organization is, in our age of specialization, a thing of the past.

A related observation is this: How can denominations and seminaries prepare the young man who expects to pursue his ministry in non-middle-class congregations? What kind of specialized staff in addition to the teaching and preaching ministry will the city congregation of the future need, where will they come from, and how shall they be trained? Denominations only now hearing with clarity the death knell of the one-man "generalist" pastorate face a wide area of exploration. The Urban Training Center in

Chicago, and the one-year postseminary internships in outstanding city churches sponsored by the United Presbyterian denomination are fragile outposts on the edge of the unknown.

REVIEW AND EVALUATION

The process of reviewing the work of the church "farther in" is easier to define than are the criteria. The state of the faith in any congregation is an elusive thing; significance and success are not identical—effectiveness is as often in the eye of the beholder as in the situation, and every church must be judged against its own potential for mission and within its specific community setting. Every congregation receiving denominational support should be visited and reviewed at least annually by representatives of the judicatory of which the congregation is a part. The regular review should move from mission to program, and only then from program to budget. A basic purpose of the visit is the renewal of the sense of oneness in mission between local congregation and denominational unit.

Beyond the housekeeping tasks and the recruiting of new members, around what claims on its ministry is this church shaping itself? How are these claims defined and determined? Should this particular church be expected to grow, and should it be expected to move toward self-support?—questions, let it be said, that do not receive an automatic *yes*. Is the membership of this congregation more in the neighborhood now than last year? More than five years ago? What programs of this local congregation relate to membership only, and what programs relate to the general community? What specific community programs has the pastor participated in during the last year? What specific services has the congregation as a corporate group rendered to the community in the past year? What specific community projects are members of the congregation participating in? What are the church plans and goals for the year to come, and how do these measure up against the check list suggested earlier in this chapter as a guide for support of an inner-city congregation? Only in the concrete response to such questions can the progress of a particular church be measured, and its staff and program needs evaluated.

The evaluation of an inner-city church is in large part the evaluation of staff leadership. This needs to be recognized by the judicatory committee making the review. Sometime during the visit the professional staff should leave the room, and a frank discussion of their leadership should ensue. There are some situations which the denomination is backing where, for the sake of the mission, the minister should be relocated. This is a touchy area, but every director of urban work or metropolitan strategy knows that some ministers fit difficult city churches as a hand fits a glove, while others do not.

Beyond the Nuts and Bolts

A TOTAL metropolitan ministry must encompass renewal and relevance within the residential parish; the establishment of ministries in the public, vocational, and leisure sectors of the society which tackle such crises as poverty and racial injustice; and the development and nurture of a denominationally accountable ecumenicity which is a servant structure rather than a structure of the churches for serving their own institutional needs. Without all these building blocks a structure for total ministry will be unbalanced and in danger of collapsing.

There are several themes which reappear consistently in this book and which give the descriptive material a bias and a tilt. The writers do not pretend that these interpretations of the *is* and the *ought* are original, but do insist they are significant as the church comes to grips with the metropolis. Indeed, they are crucial, if ministry is to lead to genuine renewal.

First, on the negative side (on which there is truth, but not the whole truth): such overworked terms as loneliness, compartmentalization, fragmentation, alienation, depersonalization, and meaninglessness point to widespread experiential realities in an urbanized social order which not only make personal wholeness and healthy intergroup relations difficult, but in their devotion to the things of this world seem to shut out ultimate concerns.

The Church is charged by God in the sometimes overwhelming metropolis to carry on a ministry of reconciliation: bringing the warring and the divided self together under the Lordship of Christ; helping the defeated to find dignity, courage, and power; uniting men in a mutual acceptance grounded in their sonship to the God and Father of us all; and, first in importance if not in the sequence of events, reconciling them to the God who is acting in their midst, even when they are unaware and uncommitted.

On the positive side: metropolis is not synonymous with individual and corporate sickness, and the Church must minister to men in their strength as well as their weakness. The majority of urban dwellers do not feel really alienated, crouching in fear in their lonely apartments, harboring a civil war within themselves, despised and rejected strangers among the uncaring crowd. Even as the Church has a divine mandate to deliver the oppressed, those who are crushed and fragmented by the city in crisis, so it must point out to the strong the source of their present deliverance. And as most men, depending on situation and circumstance, are both strong and weak, so for most men the Church must both deliver and affirm.

Second, the Incarnation, not so much as propositional truth but as Reality and Presence, must guide the Church as it goes about the business of reconciliation. The centrality of the Incarnation in mission has been stated in rather explicit theological language in the Introduction and in Chapter 1, "The Reality-Shaped Parish." The worlds, sectors, mandates, or structures (for our purposes the terms are interchangeable) where frontier ministries are now being carried on really have to do with meeting God where He is smashing the partitions that divide neighbor from neighbor, reassembling total selves from the specialized fragments, and asserting His sovereignty over the whole of life in metropolis. The exposition of the servant shape of mission (whether ecumenical, denominational, or if possible both) is simply another way of stating the same thing: namely, that the Church truly becomes the Church when it acts as the servant people of the servant God, who became one with our humanity in the person of His Son.

Third, the ministry of the residential congregation does not need to be supplanted, but it does need desperately to be supplemented. This book illustrates this theme, a recounting of the denominational and ecumenical ventures which are giving the Church a new look in metropolis, and which are not enmeshed in programming within the Church parlor and parish house.

To put the issue in question form: Where is the action in metropolis? The action in the city is certainly not institutionalized in the Church building. It goes on in the public sector, the leisure segment, the multiple worlds of work; it happens in the slum neighborhood, the towering apartment, and the sprawling suburb. Here is where the Church is striving to be relevant as it reaches out from its conventional and safe domesticity in the chapel on the corner.

The future of these new thrusts into the arenas where men work and play, where they govern, serve, and sometimes exploit one another, raises some profound questions. Undoubtedly there is a frontier here, but the nature of the unexplored territory behind the border is difficult to discern. As extensions of conventional parish life, giving focus to the lives of laymen whose togetherness is in worship and membership in the gathered parish, aiding local church pastors in the understanding of nonresidential environments and serving as a force for witness, evangelism, and social change, the relationships can be charted. Beyond this there is a vagueness.

The writers know of no ongoing congregation which is intentionally composed of, and limited to, government employees, a professional group, or workers within a particular plant or industry. Although the laymen who meet regularly around such issues as racial justice certainly can point to some marks of the Church in their concern group (at the very least a visible fellowship of believers),[4] as yet there has been no attempt to create a

---

[4] In Reformation theology the Church is present where the Word is truly preached and the sacraments properly administered. A typical statement is this one of John Calvin: ". . . the uniform characteristics of a well-ordered Church are the preaching of sound doctrine, and the pure administration of the Sacraments" (from *The Necessity of Reforming the Church*, Treatise presented to the Imperial Diet of Spires, A.D. 1544), translated from the original Latin by Henry Beveridge; *Tracts and Treatises on the Reformation of the Church*, Vol. I (Grand Rapids: William B. Eerdmans Publishing Company, 1958), p. 214. Without invalidating this

worshiping congregation in which members are pledged to militancy in achieving an integrated and color-blind society. One congregation which comes close to being a specialized congregation is the Church of the Saviour in Washington, D.C.; but even here the difference is in intensity of commitment rather than unity around an issue or within a vocational structure.

Perhaps the development of industrial, vocational, and issue-based congregations is a next step, at least on an experimental basis. And yet, would not institutionalism assert itself even in a congregation which did not use the reality of residence as a common denominator? Some kind of educational program would be needed for the children. A place would have to be found for bringing the people together, and a schedule established for worship and study. The end product might not be too different from what we now have. Which may mean that the strength of frontier thrusts lies in their informal nature, and in their continuing relationship to the residential parish with all that this means for the education and transformation of those who "stay behind."

Fourth and final, the possibility—the potential—of renewal within the Church in metropolis resides in the co-operation of the denominations. Given the vision and the will, the denominations will be able to implement a decision to live. If they fail, the Church will fail the city, this present generation, and her Lord. This assertion need not be labored further. It constitutes the underlying presupposition of this book and is implied in every example of denominational or ecumenical ministry described in its pages.

THE END IS THE BEGINNING

A *New Yorker* cartoon of a few years back highlights the never-ending conflict between hope and despair—a conflict, need-

---

basic insight of the sixteenth-century reformers, contemporary statements about the locus of the Church need to proclaim and insist that *wherever* the God of Love is served, there *too* is the Church.

less to say, which is real for the Church in metropolis. In the cartoon, two men are chained by their wrists to massive wall bolts above their heads. Huge shackles, encircling their ankles, are fastened to the base of the wall. Their bodies sag, listless and slack, against the damp stone of what is obviously a dungeon. Their clothes are disheveled, their faces unshorn, and their eyes glassy. High above their heads a solitary window opens to the world, and a single shaft of light penetrates the gathering gloom. One of the two has twisted his head toward his companion, spread-eagled on the wall beside him, and his words tell the story: "Now, here's my plan."

There are contemporary critics—not always outside the visible Church—who see the Church as an almost useless vestige in a post-Christian age: a cultural museum, if you will, where people with old-fashioned preferences can find a dusty and dreary version of security. For the skeptic or the disillusioned, plans for the development of a ministry of renewal to metropolis make about as much sense, and have about as much hope of success, as the plans of our prisoner in the cartoon.

It must be already clear that the authors do not share this God-weary pessimism. God is not dead, though men in contemporary culture are often dead to Him—which may be what Nietzsche meant, in any case. The Church is not dead or outmoded; it is a slumbering giant which is self-chained by lack of commitment rather than by any external forces. There is no dungeon except in our morbid imaginings; there is only the world of nature and of men, where the Lord of Life is ruler yet—the world for which Christ died and rose again as the firstborn of the New Humanity. The time is not twilight but early morning, the city of men is flushed with the sunlight of new opportunity, and the Church is there, called to witness and to serve in a renewed ministry to metropolis, joining God where He is busy even now in His world.

Set in Linotype Janson
Composed, printed and bound by The Haddon Craftsmen, Inc.
HARPER & ROW, PUBLISHERS, INCORPORATED